BO

BONES, MUSCLES, BLOOD
AND OTHER BODY BITS

BODY

BONES, MUSCLES, BLOOD, AND OTHER BODY BITS

By
Richard Walker

Consultant
Dr Gabrielle Murphy

A Dorling Kindersley Book

Dorling **DK** Kindersley

LONDON, NEW YORK, SYDNEY, DELHI,
PARIS, MUNICH, and JOHANNESBURG

Editor Lucy Hurst
Art Editor Ann Cannings
Senior Editor Fran Jones
Senior Art Editor Marcus James
Category Publisher Jayne Parsons
Managing Art Editor Jacquie Gulliver
Picture Researcher Brenda Clynch
DK Pictures Rachel Holt
Production Erica Rosen
DTP Designers Matthew Ibbotson,
Louise Paddick

First published in Great Britain in 2001 by
Dorling Kindersley Limited
80 Strand
London WC2R 0RL

2 4 6 8 10 9 7 5 3

Copyright © 2001 Dorling Kindersley Limited

All rights reserved. No part of this publication may be reproduced,
stored in a retrieval system, or transmitted
in any form or by any means, electronic, mechanical,
photocopying, recording, or otherwise, without prior
written permission of the copyright owner.

The CIP Catalogue record for this book is available
from the British Library

ISBN 0-7513-3078-7

Reproduced by Colourscan, Singapore
Printed and bound by L.E.G.O., Italy

See our complete catalogue at

www.dk.com

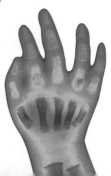

Note to Parents
Every effort has been made to ensure that the information in this book is as up-to-date as
possible at the time of going to press. The internet, by its very nature, is liable to change.
Homepages and website content is constantly being updated, as well as website addresses.
In addition, websites may contain material or links to material that may be unsuitable for
children. The publishers, therefore, cannot accept responsibility for any third party
websites or any material contained in or linked to the same or for any consequences
arising from use of the internet; nor can the publishers guarantee that any website or
urls featured in this book will be as shown. Parents are strongly advised to ensure
that access to the internet by children is supervised by a responsible adult.

CONTENTS

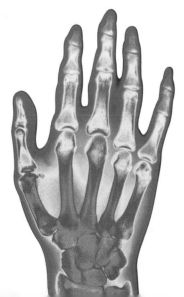

INTRODUCTION

Wherever we live, whatever we do, we all share one thing in common. A body! But, is that a reason to take our bodies for granted? Certainly not! The inside story of the human body is altogether too exciting, gruesome, and entertaining to be ignored.

And what a story it is – pieced together over many centuries by doctors, scientists, and others who were fascinated by what bodies are made of and how they work. Thanks to their efforts we now understand that the body's component parts – better known as systems – each have their own role. Put all these systems together, and you will understand the human body.

THE HEART CONSTANTLY PUMPS BLOOD AROUND YOUR BODY.

You'll find out what keeps your body upright and why it moves when you want it to. All will be revealed about the mysteries of the brain, as well as why skunks smell so unpleasant. Read on, and you'll discover how you take in life-giving oxygen, get energy from your food, as well as how urine is made or what the liver does. All this against a background of the heart pumping blood to every one of the body's cells. And there's more. You'll meet grave-robbing body snatchers, a railway worker with an iron rod through his head, Frankenstein's monster, and other fascinating characters who have all affected our knowledge of the human body.

Having found out about the body's bits, there's also time to investigate the living overcoat of protective skin that holds them all together. Not to mention the committed body defence and repair service that springs into action if anything goes wrong.

And, if this wasn't enough, we also have the means to reproduce and make new human beings to take over when our life is completed.

And there you have it. A walking, talking, breathing human body. For those of you who want to explore the subject in more detail, there are black "Log On" boxes that appear throughout the book. These will direct you to some fascinating websites where you can check out even more.

MUSCLES AND BONES SUPPORT AND MOVE YOUR BODY.

Richard Walker.

BODY BASICS

There's no doubt that we human beings are the most intelligent animals on planet Earth. We're also very curious, constantly wanting to explore the world around us, including finding out about our own bodies. We have come to understand its basic workings – right down to the tiniest cell – through a process of detective work that stretches back to our earliest ancestors.

ANCESTORS OF ALL MODERN HUMANS LIVED IN AFRICA

Early humans
Even as far back as 30,000 years ago, we know that people were aware of their bodies. Early humans recorded images of the human body as paintings on cave walls and in simple sculptures.

They were able to use their hands to paint, mould, or carve because, millions of

ONE OF THE EARLIEST HUMANS WAS AUSTRALOPITHECUS.

years before, the earliest humans – such as *Australopithecus* – had already switched from moving on all fours like their ape cousins, to standing upright on two legs. This left their hands free to do all sorts of things.

Your closest living non-human relative today – the bonobo chimpanzee – descends from a branch of the human-ape family that didn't make the move to two legs.

Same or different

If you walk down the street today, it won't take you long to realize that human bodies come in all shapes, sizes, and skin colours. Humans, like most animals, also fall into two distinct groups – females and males.

Despite these differences, all human bodies have the same basic anatomy – or structure – and work in exactly the same way, except for the parts that make us male or female. We know about anatomy because of all the body information that has been pieced together over thousands of years. Each culture has had it's own individual ideas about what made the human body tick.

Early views

The ancient Greeks, for example, thought there were four "humours" in the body – blood, yellow bile, black bile,

THESE KIDS LOOK DIFFERENT, BUT THEIR ANATOMY IS THE SAME.

and phlegm. Any imbalance in these humours would make someone ill. Especially someone with no sense of humour!

Claudius Galen (AD 129–201), a Greek doctor, took these ideas on and became a star physician in Rome. There was a ban, unfortunately, on dissecting (cutting up) humans, so he used pigs, goats, and sheep, assuming that their anatomy would be the same. It wasn't! But Galen was so convincing that everyone accepted his ideas, many of which were wrong.

After his death, Galen's views about the body remained unchallenged for more than 1,300 years. People who dared to criticize Galen's books were either laughed at or punished.

THE FOUR HUMOURS

PHLEGM

BLOOD

BLACK BILE

YELLOW BILE

New ideas

By the 16th century, however, Galen's beliefs were starting to be questioned. Two people – Leonardo da Vinci (1452–1519) and Andreas Vesalius (1514–64) – played a key part in waving goodbye to the past.

Leonardo was a brilliant artist and scientist. He dissected more than 30 bodies by candlelight in the Santo Spirito mortuary. Using his own – not Galen's – observations and incredible technical skills, Leonardo drew what he actually saw in a thousand accurate drawings of the body.

Vesalius, a doctor, was tired of other doctors pretending not to notice that the insides of bodies looked nothing like the pictures in dusty old books. So he started stealing the bodies of executed criminals, taking them home, and cutting them up to see how they were put together. Some bodies were kept for weeks, so he must have had understanding neighbours!

In 1543 Vesalius published his notes in a book called *De Humanis Corporis Fabrica* which, for those of you who don't read Latin, means *The Structure of the*

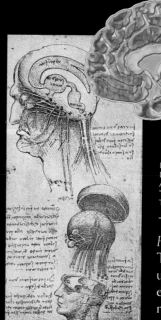

LEONARDO'S DRAWINGS AND A MODERN SCAN "CUTTING" THROUGH THE BRAIN

Human Body. There was uproar, but eventually it was realized Vesalius was right and Galen was wrong.

Body snatchers

In 16th-century England, doctors wanting to find out about, or teach, anatomy were only allowed to use the bodies of executed criminals. But the sudden interest in anatomy meant that the supply of dead bodies just couldn't keep up with demand.

It didn't take long for some bright spark to realize that there was money to be made in selling dead bodies to unscrupulous doctors. Gangs of "body snatchers" would dig up freshly buried corpses from graveyards, and deliver them to medical schools in return for cash.

In the 1820s, two Scottish body snatchers were getting tired of digging up bodies. William Burke and William Hare decided to murder people instead, supplying fresh corpses to their doctor client. It wasn't long before they were caught. Hare betrayed Burke, who was hanged and his body was sent for dissection!

Seeing inside a body

Until the end of the 19th century, the best way that doctors could see inside the body – living or dead – was to cut it open. But in 1895, things changed. German scientist

> ## WEIRD WORLD
> EVEN WILLIAM HARVEY – THE DOCTOR WHO EXPLAINED BLOOD CIRCULATION IN 1628 – WAS REDUCED TO DISSECTING HIS FATHER AND SISTER TO KEEP HIS RESEARCH GOING.

Wilhelm Roentgen found that X-rays could pass through soft things, like skin and muscle, but not hard stuff, like bones. He shook up the medical world when he discovered that, by projecting X-rays through the body onto photographic film, he could produce a picture of the inside of the body showing bones but not soft tissues. Doctors could now see fractures, and weird things like bullets and swallowed coins.

More high-tech methods were invented in the 1970s and '80s. One of them, called MRI (magnetic resonance imaging), combines magnetism and radiowaves to produce "slices" through the body without spilling a drop of blood. Another, called ultrasound, bounces sound waves off body parts and uses the echo to make a picture of what's happening inside. Because it is very safe, ultrasound is used to

BODY SNATCHERS AT WORK

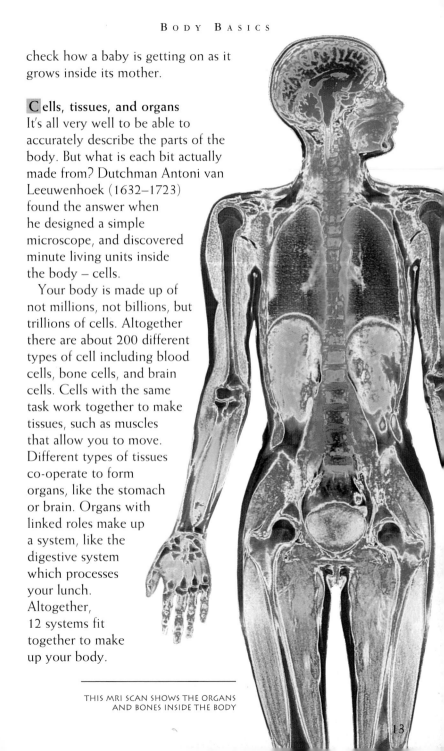

check how a baby is getting on as it grows inside its mother.

Cells, tissues, and organs

It's all very well to be able to accurately describe the parts of the body. But what is each bit actually made from? Dutchman Antoni van Leeuwenhoek (1632–1723) found the answer when he designed a simple microscope, and discovered minute living units inside the body – cells.

Your body is made up of not millions, not billions, but trillions of cells. Altogether there are about 200 different types of cell including blood cells, bone cells, and brain cells. Cells with the same task work together to make tissues, such as muscles that allow you to move. Different types of tissues co-operate to form organs, like the stomach or brain. Organs with linked roles make up a system, like the digestive system which processes your lunch. Altogether, 12 systems fit together to make up your body.

THIS MRI SCAN SHOWS THE ORGANS
AND BONES INSIDE THE BODY

MEAT AND BONES

Without its supporting skeleton, the body would be as useful as a tent without poles. In other words, you would be spread out on the ground unable to find the remote control! To work properly, bones need meat, or muscles. Hundreds of skeletal muscles pull on your bones so you can walk, write, and do thousands of other things. Between them, muscles and bones shape, support, and move your body.

HALF MUSCLE, HALF BONE

BY WEIGHT, BONE IS STRONGER THAN STEEL

Bony frame
Did you know that your skeleton has 206 bones? Some of them are tiny, like the rice grain-sized stirrup bone deep inside your ear. Others, like the mighty femur in your thigh, are big and strong enough to carry your weight. Inside your flexible but strong bony framework, soft organs like the brain and heart are protected from damage.

LOG ON...
www.last-word.com/
lastword/body.html

Your bones also provide somewhere to anchor muscles, so that you can tug on them and make your body jump, dance, and run when you want it to.

What bones are made of

People often think of bones as being dry, dusty, and dead, because that is how we usually see them. But bones inside a living person are nothing like that. They are one-third water, full of nerves and blood vessels, and contain cells that are forever rebuilding and reshaping your bones. Living bones are made of mineral salts for hardness, and collagen fibres for strength. After death, the collagen rots away leaving just a hard but brittle bone-shaped shell behind.

For a closer look inside bones, you would need a microscope. This would show that bones are made up of different bits. The outer layer of bone has tubes of bony tissue running along it – like rolled-up newspaper – that give it strength. Because they are crammed together these tubes are called compact bone.

Further inside, bone looks like honeycomb. Struts and spaces make this spongy bone strong but light. If your bones weren't spongy, they would be so heavy you wouldn't be able to move your body.

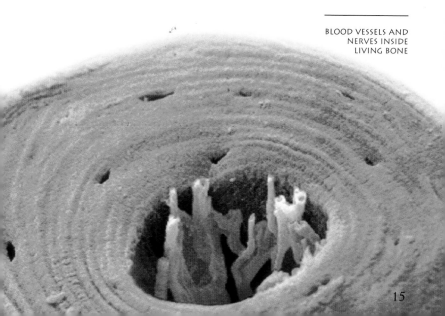

BLOOD VESSELS AND
NERVES INSIDE
LIVING BONE

15

WHEN A PERSON DOES YOGA, IT HELPS TO MAKE THEIR JOINTS MORE FLEXIBLE.

Blood factory

As well as supporting you, bones also make the red blood cells that whizz around your body. The blood cell factory is found in bone marrow, the jelly-like stuff inside bones. There are two types of marrow. Fatty, yellow marrow – much loved by dogs when they chew bones – doesn't make blood cells. But red marrow – found inside your shoulder blades, ribs, breastbone, and pelvis – does. The high-speed red

EVERY SECOND, BONE MARROW MAKES 2,000,000 RED BLOOD CELLS

It may seem a bit odd, but when you were much younger and smaller you had more bones in your skeleton than you do now. A newborn baby has more than 300 "bones" making up its skeleton. In fact, some of these "bones" aren't very hard. They are made of cartilage, the stuff that makes your nose and ear bendy. Then as you get older, real bone replaces cartilage to make your bones longer and stronger. And some bones join together. That's why you've ended up with fewer than you started with.

marrow production line churns out exactly the right number of red blood cells needed to replace the worn-out ones.

THESE HAND X-RAYS SHOW HOW BONES (PURPLE) REPLACE CARTILAGE BY THE TIME YOU ARE AN ADULT.

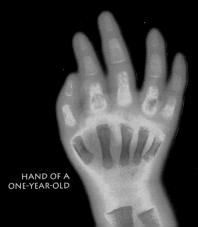

HAND OF A ONE-YEAR-OLD

Moving joints

Pick up your favourite food item and, without bending your arm at all, pop it into your mouth. Impossible, isn't it? So, thank goodness for joints – the bendy points in the skeleton where bones meet and make movement possible. Some joints, like those in the hip and shoulder, allow all-round movement. Others, like the hinge joint in the knee, only allow movement back and forth. To stop lots of grinding noises when you move, most joints have thick, oily liquid inside which makes them work smoothly, like a well-oiled machine.

The skull has a different kind of joint. Press your fingers against the sides of your head.

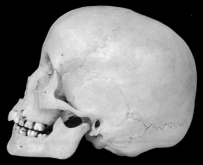

THE SUTURES IN THIS SIX-YEAR-OLD'S SKULL FIT TOGETHER LIKE A JIGSAW.

You should find – unless you're an alien – that you can't squeeze it inwards. That's because, although your skull is made up of 22 separate bones, the joints between them don't move. Sutures, as these joints are called, fit tightly together

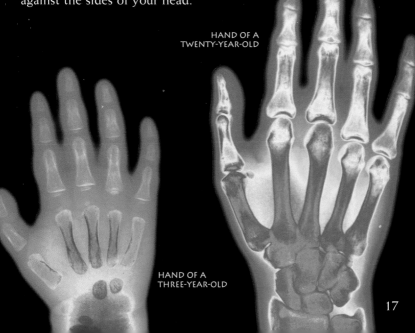

HAND OF A TWENTY-YEAR-OLD

HAND OF A THREE-YEAR-OLD

17

like jigsaw pieces. This makes the skull really strong, ideal for protecting your squashy brain and giving your face its shape. In fact, there is one skull bone – the lower jaw – that does move. This is fortunate, otherwise you wouldn't be able to open your mouth to eat your lunch.

While joints may be great for making the skeleton flexible, without ligaments they would be quite useless. Ligaments are strong – but slightly stretchy – straps that hold bones together at joints, like in the knee. They stop bones moving too much or in the wrong directions. Sometimes, if you push your bones too far,

LIGAMENTS (BROWN) AROUND THE KNEE JOINT HOLD IT TOGETHER.

they pop out of their joints and tear their ligaments – the shoulder is a common place for this to happen. Doctors call this dislocation and it needs their expert skills to carefully manoeuvre the bones back into place without too much nerve pinching or tissue crunching. Ouch!

Handy hands

So, if you put all this together, you can see how important your bones, joints, and ligaments are. Your hands are a good example. Ever since our hairy ancestors moved from walking on four legs to two, humans have had their hands free to do all sorts of things. Writing a letter, tying shoe laces, or lifting a heavy weight, are only a few of the many tasks your hands can perform. Why are they so versatile?

• Each hand is made of 27 small bones, making it very flexible.

• Your thumb can touch the tips of the other four fingers.

• Some 20 muscles in the forearm pull on hand bones. They do this by using long tendons (you can see them on the back of the hand or under the wrist), to produce hundreds of different types of movements, from a powerful grip to the most delicate touch.

Because your bones remain behind after you are long gone, people have always been able to see what a skeleton looks like. But finding out about muscles was a more gruesome task until recently. Let's see how it was done.

THE WORD "MUSCLE" COMES FROM EARLY ROMANS WHO BELIEVED A CONTRACTING MUSCLE LOOKED LIKE A LITTLE MOUSE – "MUSCULUS" – RUNNING ABOUT UNDER THE SKIN.

S **how us your muscles!**
You wouldn't have wanted to be a criminal centuries ago, in case you were flayed! This messy process involved carefully cutting away a person's skin to expose the skeletal muscles underneath. This was very useful for doctors trying to teach their students how muscles worked.

So what is muscle made of? Muscle is made up of cells called fibres. Unlike most body cells, they are not small and compact, but instead, are long and packed with special stringy filaments. These filaments work together to make the muscle fibre contract, or get shorter.

WAX MODEL, MADE IN 1785 IN ITALY SHOWS THE MUSCLES OF THE UPPER BODY.

They do this when your brain – which is the boss – says so, by sending nerve signals. If the fibres in a muscle contract, the whole muscle gets shorter, and that part of the body moves.

Meat market

To imagine what your muscles look like, take a trip to the meat counter at your local supermarket – vegetarians beware! Those red chunks of meat are the skeletal muscles of sheep, cows, and other animals. The "meat" from your own body makes up more than 40 per cent of your body weight.

ACHILLES' MUM DIPPING HIM INTO THE RIVER STYX TO TRY AND MAKE HIM IMMORTAL.

TRICEPS   BICEPS

TRICEPS AND BICEPS WORK TOGETHER TO MOVE YOUR ARM UP AND DOWN.

Tendons

Just above your heel, at the back of your leg, you should be able to feel a fairly solid ridge of tissue. That's your Achilles tendon. Like other tendons, it's a tough cord that links muscles to bones.

Achilles was a Greek hero. When he was young, his mother held him by the heel and dipped him into the River Styx to make him immortal. This worked well until he was shot in his undipped heel with an arrow and died. From this sad tale we get the name Achilles tendon. Through it, the calf muscles pull on the ankle bone to point the foot downwards.

Push and pull muscles

Pulling may be a speciality of muscles, but pushing certainly

20

isn't. Muscle fibres use energy to contract, but then they just relax to return to their normal length. So, if you want to bend and straighten your arm, for example, you need at least two muscles: one (the biceps) to pull the bones one way to bend, and one (the triceps) to pull the other way and straighten. This arrangement of muscles is found all over your body. Some pull bones one way, and others in the opposite direction.

A number of muscles work all the time that you are awake. Those in your back, neck, and buttocks, for example, stay partially contracted to hold you upright and give you posture. This muscle tone, as it is known, disappears when you fall asleep. That's why a sleeping body gets all floppy.

P ulling faces
Wherever you go in the world a smile means the same

thing. So does a frown for that matter. More than 20 small muscles around the eyes, nose, and mouth produce the facial expressions that show when you are happy or annoyed or, for that matter, frightened, sad, angry, surprised, or disgusted.

Face muscles are a bit unusual because instead of pulling on bones, they tug at the skin on your face. Just a tiny twitch can alter your facial expression to reveal a subtle change in mood. In fact, the only way to keep your feelings to yourself is to put a paper bag over your head!

THIS MAORI MAN'S FACIAL EXPRESSION SHOWS HE IS READY TO FIGHT.

WEIRD WORLD
TONGUES ARE MADE OF MUSCLE TOO. TONGUE MUSCLES MAKE IT THICKER, THINNER, LONGER, OR SHORTER AS WELL AS PULLING IT IN OR PUSHING IT OUT , HELPING YOU TO SPEAK, SWALLOW... OR LOOK AGGRESSIVE!

SENSATIONAL SENSES

At this very second, millions of tiny sensors are sending a stream of messages to your brain to tell it what's happening inside and outside your body. Touch sensors – they include pain, pressure, heat, and cold sensors too – are found all over the place. The other four senses – sight, hearing, taste, smell – have sensors inside special organs: the eyes, ears, tongue, and nose.

YOUR EYES CONTAIN 70 PER CENT OF YOUR BODY'S SENSORS

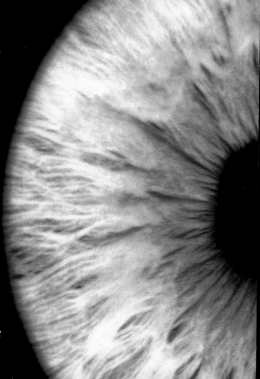

Vision on
Of all the senses, vision is probably the most important. It gives you a moving picture of the outside world. Being able to see means that you can read this book, find your way to the fridge, play football, and recognize your friends. To make vision happen, your eyes detect light, and your brain produces the pictures.

Like hollow golf balls, your eyes sit protected inside bony sockets in the skull. The inner lining of each eyeball is a thin layer called the retina that is packed with millions of light sensors. Light, reflected from things around you, zooms into the eye through the clear bit at the front – the cornea which covers the iris and pupil – and is focused by the lens onto the retina. As light patterns hit the sensors they send signals to the back of your brain. Here the messages are

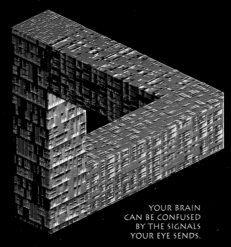

YOUR BRAIN CAN BE CONFUSED BY THE SIGNALS YOUR EYE SENDS.

sorted out and you "see" what is in front of you.

Eye tricks

Your brain uses all sorts of clues to make pictures from the stream of signals sent from your eyes. But sometimes the clues aren't very clear, so the brain isn't really quite sure what to make of the

THE PUPIL GETS WIDER IN DIM LIGHT AND NARROWER IN BRIGHT LIGHT.

THE IRIS RANGES IN COLOUR.

23

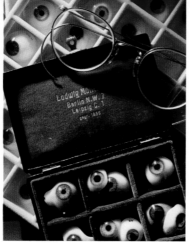

GLASSES HELP EYES FOCUS PROPERLY,
WHILE GLASS EYES REPLACE MISSING ONES.

are sent rippling through the air. These vibrations wobble their way into the inner ear where a snail shell-shaped thing called the cochlea sits.

Inside the cochlea are about 15,000 sound sensors, with lots of "hairs" sprouting from the top of them. As sound waves bounce in, they squash these hairs, and make the sensors send a message to

OPENING
OF THE
EAR CANAL

information it receives. This is how optical illusions happen. Your brain has been tricked!

Hear hear!

You may call those two flappy things on the side of your head ears, but in fact they're just one part of the sense organs that detect sounds. The main bits of the ears are hidden inside your skull bones. To find them you'd have to travel down the ear canal – the entrance is the hole in the middle of the flappy bit or pinna – past the ear drum, over the tiny ear bones or ossicles, and into the inner ear.

When a baby cries, the orchestra tunes up, or your sister shouts at you, vibrations called sound waves

WHEN SOUND WAVES ENTER YOUR EAR, THESE TINY HAIRS MOVE, CAUSING NERVES TO CARRY A MESSAGE TO YOUR BRAIN.

OSSICLES

COCHLEA

EAR DRUM

B alanced view

Let's add an extra sense here, that's related to hearing. That sense is balance, the one that stops you falling over and tells you whether you are standing on your head, or not.

Sensors inside your inner ear – next to the cochlea – tell your brain whether you are moving forwards, backwards, or sideways, and whether you are upright, lying

your brain, via nerves. Your brain is so smart it can tell the difference between a high-pitched scream or a low-pitched groan, the loudness of a rock band, or the quietness of a pin dropping.

MODEL SHOWING
INSIDE THE
HUMAN EAR

25

down, or upside down. With extra messages from your eyes, feet, and muscles, your brain gets enough information to tweak your muscles, move your body, and keep you balanced.

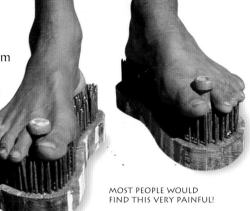

MOST PEOPLE WOULD FIND THIS VERY PAINFUL!

What a pain!

Although pain hurts, it's still a useful sensation. It's a warning signal that says your body may be injured. Of the three million pain sensors dotted around the body, most are in your skin. These skin sensors make you feel sharp pains, like when you prick your finger with a pin. Pain sensors inside your body produce longer-lasting aches like sore muscles or stomach cramps.

Stress can make the body produce its own natural painkillers. That's why soldiers can be badly wounded in battle but feel nothing – until the fighting is over, and the painkillers wear off.

Touchy feely

Apart from pain detectors, there's a whole brigade of touch sensors in your skin. Some detect light touch, others vibrations, and yet others pick up different amounts of pressure. You can tell just by feeling the difference, for example, between velvet and sandpaper. Pressure sensors will let you know whether it's a friend standing on your foot, or an elephant (unless your best friend is an elephant!). And there's more. Grab a handful of ice cubes, and cold receptors soon let your brain know that your fingers are starting to freeze. Or, when you accidentally stick your foot in a bath that's too hot, heat sensors scream at you to pull your foot out before it cooks.

But, here's something

WEIRD WORLD

SOME PEOPLE WHO HAVE HAD A PART OF THEIR ARM OR LEG AMPUTATED CAN STILL FEEL PAIN OR ITCHING IN THE MISSING BIT. THIS IS CALLED PHANTOM PAIN BECAUSE IT'S A GHOSTLY REMINDER OF WHAT USED TO BE THERE.

LOG ON...
www.KidsHealth.org/kid/

strange. Why is it that when you wear clothes they don't feel scratchy as they rub against your skin? You feel clothes as you put them on, but very quickly the sensation fades. Your brain just "ignores" the signals coming from the touch sensors in your skin. Scientists call this habituation. Without it, daily life would be very itchy and uncomfortable.

Good taste

Your tongue has touch sensors too (although fingers are better when you're feeling for that missing coin down the back of the sofa!). It can detect heat – handy for preventing burning when you eat hot food – and has cold detectors, so you can feel the iciness of ice cream. It even has pain sensors. These can be triggered by a chemical in chilli peppers called capsaicin. That's why chillies feel painfully hot. But, most important of all, your tongue can taste.

Look at your tongue in a mirror and you will see lots of tiny bumps, called papillae.

A MAGNIFIED VIEW OF THE SURFACE OF A TONGUE. TASTE BUDS SIT AT THE BASE OF THE BIG RED ROUND PAPILLAE.

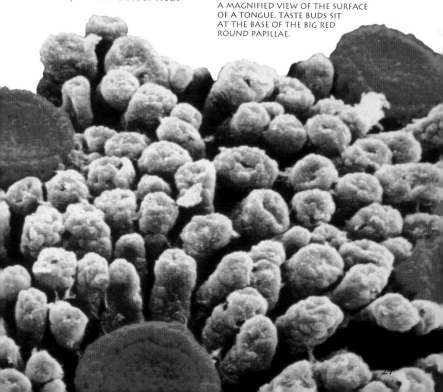

Under the microscope some of these papillae look round, while some are pointed. About 10,000 taste buds – the sensors that detect tastes – are tucked down the sides of the round papillae. When you eat

adults can pick out 10,000 different odours, and children do even better. Smell works in the same basic way as taste. Breathe in through your nose, and odour molecules dissolve in the watery mucus (the stuff that

THE TONGUE DETECTS FOUR TASTES – SWEET, SOUR, SALTY, AND BITTER

something, taste molecules dissolve in saliva, and it's these that are picked up by the taste buds.

BITTER

SOUR, LIKE LEMONS

SALTY

SWEET

AREAS OF THE TONGUE RECOGNIZE DIFFERENT TASTES.

S mell this

When it comes to sensitivity, smell leaves taste far behind. It's an amazing 20,000 times more sensitive. What's more,

comes out when you sneeze) inside your nose. When these molecules hit smell detectors in the top of your nasal cavity – the space inside your nose – they fire off signals to the brain.

Smell and taste work together so that you can appreciate flavours. The nose is the boss in this partnership. If you have a blocked nose, food flavours become so bland that, blindfolded, you'd have problems telling what you are eating. Sometimes the two senses are in conflict, as people who eat durians soon discover. This southeast Asian fruit tastes simply delicious but smells like a public toilet on a hot day.

Apart from letting you appreciate the aromas of good food and fresh flowers, smell is useful in other ways. It helps you steer clear of stinking,

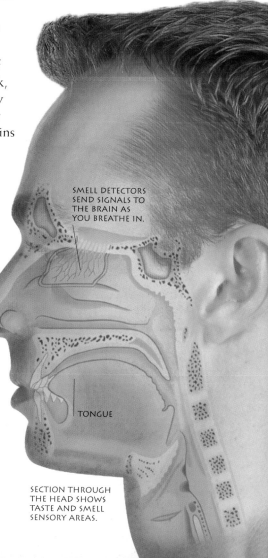

money on the phone bill!). Even more quirky is telekinesis, a feature of ESP that lets you move things just by thinking about it. But, most scientists don't believe the evidence. They're sticking with five senses – for now!

rotten foods, and warns of possible dangers, such as smoke and burning. And if you get sprayed by a skunk, burn your clothes, and stay away from your friends for a week. Skunk spray contains mercaptan, the smelliest substance in the world. Humans can detect mercaptans when there is just one solitary molecule of the revolting stuff diluted in 30 billion molecules of air. Phew!

F ive...or six?

So much for the five senses. But do you have an extra, sixth, sense? Well, some people think they do. Often called extrasensory perception or ESP, this mysterious sixth sense apparently allows you to use telepathy to read people's minds or to send them thoughts without speaking (that should save

SMELL DETECTORS SEND SIGNALS TO THE BRAIN AS YOU BREATHE IN.

TONGUE

SECTION THROUGH THE HEAD SHOWS TASTE AND SMELL SENSORY AREAS.

BRAIN POWER

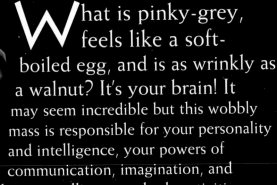

What is pinky-grey, feels like a soft-boiled egg, and is as wrinkly as a walnut? It's your brain! It may seem incredible but this wobbly mass is responsible for your personality and intelligence, your powers of communication, imagination, and memory, as well as controlling most body activities. Being soft makes the brain vulnerable, but luckily it sits well protected inside the bony dome of the skull.

STEVE MARTIN FELL IN LOVE WITH A BRAIN IN THE FILM "THE MAN WITH TWO BRAINS".

Protected brain
Your soft brain floats safely inside your skull, cushioned and nourished by a watery substance called cerebrospinal fluid. The fluid absorbs knocks that might otherwise damage the brain. This protection hasn't stopped curious people investigating the brain. Back in the Stone Age, trepanning – as cutting skull holes is called – was done regularly. Exposing the brain was meant to cure headaches and mental illness.

THE REMAINS OF A 4,000-YEAR-OLD TREPANNED SKULL

Left and right sides
Today, a lot more is understood about the brain. Its main section is the big wrinkly bit called the cerebrum. Scientists have worked out that different parts of the cerebrum are involved in vision, hearing, movement, touch, speech, and so on. If you look at the cerebrum you can see that it is divided into two halves called the left and right cerebral hemispheres. The left hemisphere controls the right side of the body, and the right

hemisphere the left side. Usually the left hemisphere is dominant, which makes most people right-handed. The left hemisphere also controls speech, writing, numbers, and problem solving, while the right hemisphere deals with art, music, and recognizing faces.

Changed personality

The functions of the brain are also divided by area within each hemisphere. We know, for example, that the front of the brain is mostly responsible for personality because of

an accident involving Phineas Gage, a US railway construction worker. In 1848, an explosion accidentally drove a 2.5 cm- (1 inch-) diameter iron bar through Gage's left cheek bone, the front of his brain, and then out through the top of his skull. Remarkably, Gage survived. But he became bad-tempered, lazy, and rude when before he had been a good worker and well-liked. His personality had completely

THE BRAIN, SEEN FROM ABOVE, SHOWS THE LEFT AND RIGHT SIDES OF THE CEREBRUM.

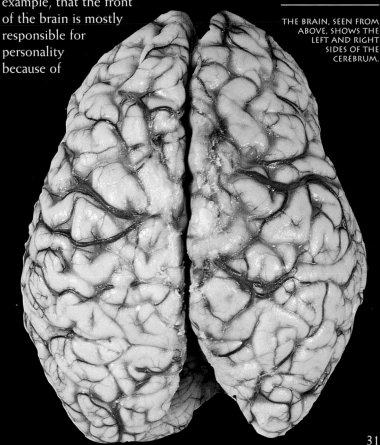

changed. Gage's misfortune showed that the brain has different parts, and spurred many scientists on to do more research.

B rain connections

You'll be pleased to know that your brain is so powerful and complex, it leaves computers far behind. Why? Well, inside the brain there are about

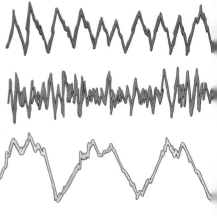

100 billion nerve cells, known as neurons. Neurons are slightly different from other body cells because they specialize in carrying electrical signals called nerve impulses at very high speed. Each one of these neurons has connections with hundreds or even

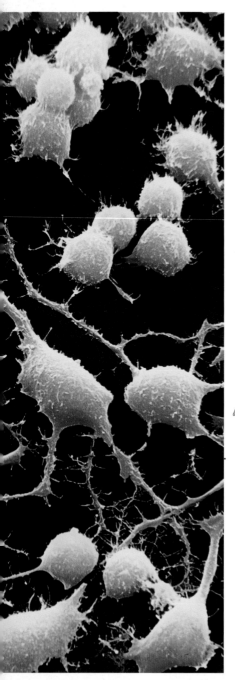

INSIDE YOUR BRAIN, NEURONS LIKE THESE PROCESS AND PASS ON IMPULSES AND INFORMATION AT LIGHTNING SPEED.

thousands of other neurons that together produce a massive communication network. This receives messages from sensors, for example from inside the eye so you can see where you're going. It sends out instructions, so you can do things like walk in a straight line, and digest your lunch. And the network analyses and stores information so you think and remember.

between neurons. So people can be really bright – or not – regardless of their brain size.

LOG ON...
www.soton.ac.uk/~jrc3/chudler/neurok.html

B rain waves

Having a brain wave usually means that you've had a brilliant idea. But your brain actually gives off brain waves

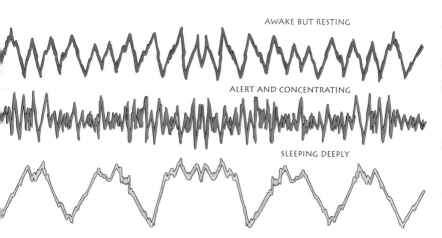

AWAKE BUT RESTING

ALERT AND CONCENTRATING

SLEEPING DEEPLY

BRAIN WAVES PRODUCED BY ELECTRICAL SIGNALS DURING DIFFERENT ACTIVITIES

I ntelligence

The connections between all those billions of brain cells are also responsible for your intelligence. You might think men are more intelligent than women, because an average man's brain weighs 1.35 kg (3 lb) and a woman's weighs 1.25 kg (2.75 lb). But they aren't – intelligence does not depend on brain size, but on the number of connections

all the time, day and night. These are produced by the billions of electrical signals that flash between your brain's neurons every second. Brain waves vary depending on whether you are resting, really concentrating, or sleeping at the back of the class.

Why do you need to spend one-third of your life asleep?

Scientists think sleep gives your brain time to sort out the previous day's experiences, and gives your body a chance to rest. Without sleep, you would soon become weak and ill.

Sleeping and waking are part of a natural 24-hour rhythm controlled by the brain. This natural clock explains why you feel pretty tired at 3 a.m. and – hopefully – bright and

and a part of the left cerebral hemisphere sends instructions to the vocal cords in your throat so that you make sounds.

But there are other ways of getting your feelings across. Gestures and body language – the way your body is positioned when you talk or listen to people – are both important. The look on your face can also reveal how you feel.

Imagine that

How dull life would be if you weren't able to think up new ideas for yourself. Writing a story,

THIS PART OF YOUR BRAIN TELLS YOUR VOCAL CORDS TO MAKE SOUNDS AND COMMUNICATE.

alert at 10 a.m. These rhythms are easily disturbed, for example, by a long-distance flight to a different time zone.

THIS PART RECEIVES AND INTERPRETS NERVE SIGNALS FROM YOUR EAR AS YOU LISTEN.

Making contact

When you are wide awake, your versatile brain lets you communicate with other human beings. The way most humans do this is by speaking a common language. You think about what you want to say,

painting a picture, working out some new dance steps, or just explaining something in a different way, all depend on your brain's ability to be imaginative and creative. Most conscious creative thoughts and ideas come from the right cerebral hemisphere, the half that also deals with appreciating music and art. But imagination can also involve unconscious thoughts. These come from deep inside the brain, and are where your basic emotions such as

Memory bank

Where would you be without your memory? You wouldn't be able to remember where you took your last holiday, learn anything new, recognize your friends, or even say something understandable. So it's a good

YOUR BRAIN HOLDS BILLIONS OF MEMORIES, SOME FOR LIFE

happiness and sadness also arise. Imagination is just another part of your intelligence, which also includes being able to solve problems, learn, and remember.

thing that your brain can sort out the information it receives, store what it wants to keep, and

VINCENT VAN GOGH (1853–90) USED HIS IMAGINATION TO CREATE THIS PAINTING.

recall what it needs when it needs it. A very simple way to look at memory is to divide it into two parts. Working – or short-term – memory briefly stores what's happening to you right now, like reading this

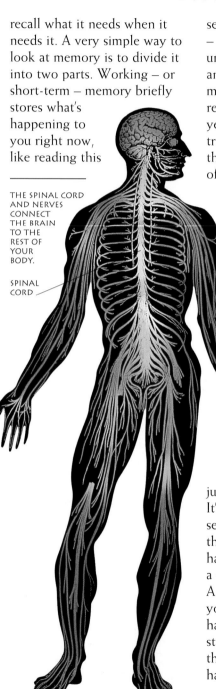

THE SPINAL CORD
AND NERVES
CONNECT
THE BRAIN
TO THE
REST OF
YOUR
BODY.

SPINAL
CORD

sentence. Selected information – such as a scary film or an unusual phrase – is passed on and stored in long-term memory. This can then be recalled days, months, or even years later. Memories may be triggered by sights or smells that are stored in different parts of the brain.

What a nerve!

Your brain links to the rest of your body via the spinal cord and nerves. Finger-thick and squashy, the spinal cord runs through your backbone and relays messages to and from the brain. Nerves pop out of the spinal cord, and then branch out to carry nerve impulses to and from all parts of your body.

But the spinal cord is more than just an extension of the brain. It's also responsible for spilt-second responses called reflexes that protect you from everyday hazards. Catch your finger on a cactus, and what happens? A nerve impulse zooms up to your spinal cord, and – without having to think about it – straight back to an arm muscle that immediately pulls your hand away.

Losing your head

For a long time, a regular method of execution was beheading. Ouch! But, could the brain survive if its blood supply from the heart was cut off, and spinal cord connection severed? You may think it's impossible to answer this, because a headless person would be dead and unable to comment. But one enterprising French doctor decided to find out. In 1905, Dr Beaurieux looked on as the guillotine

WEIRD WORLD

IS A HEADACHE A PAIN IN THE BRAIN? NO IT ISN'T. YOUR BRAIN DOESN'T HAVE ANY SENSORS OF ITS OWN, SO IT CAN'T ACTUALLY "FEEL" PAIN. HEADACHES ARE COMMONLY CAUSED BY TENSION IN HEAD MUSCLES AND MEMBRANES SURROUNDING THE BRAIN.

sliced off the head of the notorious murderer Languille. When, seconds later, Beaurieux shouted "Languille!" at the severed head something weird happened. Three times in 30 seconds, the murderer's eyelids opened and he fixed his focused eyes on the doctor's.

Brain for life

Languille's brain must have been working for him to hear the doctor's voice and open his eyelids. The rest of his body was completely lifeless. This shows that the brain can survive without the body for a few seconds, but your body just can't survive without your brain.

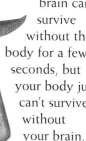

A GRUESOME BEHEADING

37

BLOOD SUPPLY

E veryone knows what blood looks
like, but do you know what it does?
Bodies are made of trillions of cells, and each
one demands a non-stop supply of food and
oxygen. In order to provide this service, the heart pumps
blood around the body – through blood
vessels – in the circulation system.

C rimson liquid

Thick, red, and runny, blood
consists of billions of cells
floating in a liquid called
plasma. Most of these cells
are the red blood cells
that give blood its colour.
The rest are either white
blood cells that hunt down
and kill invading germs before
they cause trouble, or platelets
that lay on a 24-hour repair
service. If you cut yourself
and damage a blood vessel,
for example, the platelets stick
together and plug the leak. Then
you'd see a scab form over the
plug to help the cut heal.

S upply service

Blood works like a delivery
service – supplying oxygen, food,
and other goodies to the body's
cells, and removing waste like
carbon dioxide, before it poisons
the whole body. Blood also
spreads heat around, so that

PLATELET

38

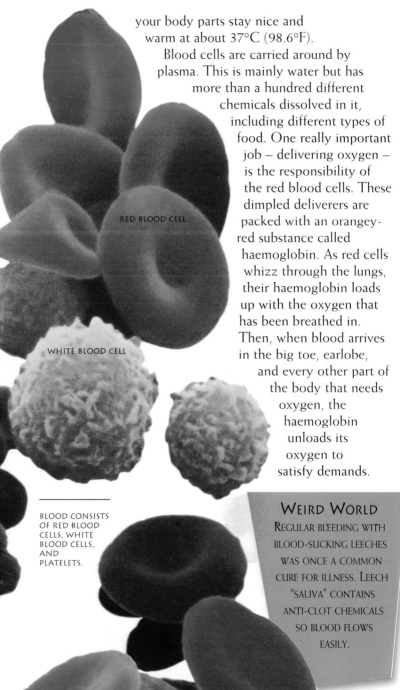

your body parts stay nice and warm at about 37°C (98.6°F). Blood cells are carried around by plasma. This is mainly water but has more than a hundred different chemicals dissolved in it, including different types of food. One really important job – delivering oxygen – is the responsibility of the red blood cells. These dimpled deliverers are packed with an orangey-red substance called haemoglobin. As red cells whizz through the lungs, their haemoglobin loads up with the oxygen that has been breathed in. Then, when blood arrives in the big toe, earlobe, and every other part of the body that needs oxygen, the haemoglobin unloads its oxygen to satisfy demands.

RED BLOOD CELL

WHITE BLOOD CELL

BLOOD CONSISTS OF RED BLOOD CELLS, WHITE BLOOD CELLS, AND PLATELETS.

WEIRD WORLD

REGULAR BLEEDING WITH BLOOD-SUCKING LEECHES WAS ONCE A COMMON CURE FOR ILLNESS. LEECH "SALIVA" CONTAINS ANTI-CLOT CHEMICALS SO BLOOD FLOWS EASILY.

Pumping heart

To do its job, blood needs to be pumped around the body. This is the task of the heart. People once thought that the heart gave us our personality and feelings. We now know it is the brain that does that.

Used-up, or oxygen-poor, blood enters the heart from large veins. It goes first into the right atrium, which squeezes it into the right ventricle, and then onto the lungs to be refreshed with oxygen. It returns to the left side of the heart, through the left atrium, and into the left ventricle. The heart then pumps oxygen-rich blood to where it is needed – that is, everywhere in the body.

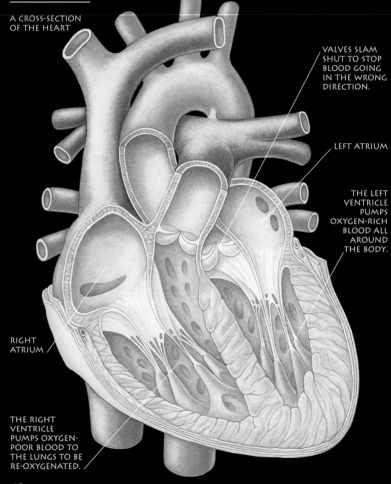

A CROSS-SECTION OF THE HEART

VALVES SLAM SHUT TO STOP BLOOD GOING IN THE WRONG DIRECTION.

LEFT ATRIUM

THE LEFT VENTRICLE PUMPS OXYGEN-RICH BLOOD ALL AROUND THE BODY.

RIGHT ATRIUM

THE RIGHT VENTRICLE PUMPS OXYGEN-POOR BLOOD TO THE LUNGS TO BE RE-OXYGENATED.

Heart beat

As you sit and read this, your heart is probably beating about 70 times each minute. A built-in pacemaker keeps it beating at the right rate. If you a car crash and used it to replace the heart of a man in his 50s who was dying from heart disease. Sadly, the man lived for just 18 days, but Dr Barnard had showed that a

HEART MUSCLE NEVER TIRES AND NEVER TAKES A BREAK

exercise, the rate speeds up to make sure your muscles get more blood. During each heartbeat, both sides of your heart relax to draw in blood, and then contract to squeeze blood either to the lungs or the rest of the body. With each beat, flappy heart valves close to stop blood going in the wrong direction, and make the thumping sounds you hear if you listen to someone's chest.

New hearts

Sometimes hearts don't work as well as they should, and need replacing. Today, heart transplants are quite routine, and can give people with serious heart disease a new lease of life. This operation was first pioneered in 1967 by South African surgeon Christiaan Barnard. He took the heart from a young woman who had just died in

heart transplant was possible.

Giving blood

A heart is not the only thing that can be moved from one body to another. We know how vital blood is – if a person loses too much, they die. The

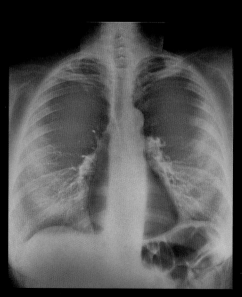

THE HEART (RED) SITS INSIDE YOUR CHEST, PROTECTED BY THE STERNUM AND RIBS.

idea of replacing lost blood by transfusion – taking blood from a donor (giver) and transfering it into a patient – was first considered in the 17th century. Attempts were made with blood from sheep, dogs, and then – sensibly – other humans. Some transfusions succeeded, but others made patients very ill or just killed them.

No-one was really sure what was going on until Austrian doctor Karl Landsteiner (1868–1943) showed that there are four different types of blood. He called them A, B, AB, and O. Landsteiner also showed that if you gave the wrong type of blood to someone – for example if you give a person with type A blood a transfusion of type B blood – their red blood cells would stick together. If this happened, small blood vessels could become blocked and the

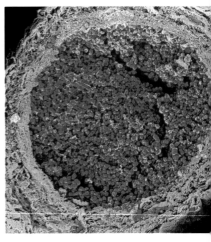

CROSS-SECTION OF A BLOOD-FILLED ARTERY

patient would die. Thanks to Landsteiner's discoveries, millions of safe blood transfusions now take place every day.

T ube transport

It's great having a pump and the right kind of blood, but how does blood get everywhere it is needed? Fortunately, a massive tubular

MODEL SHOWS THE ARTERIES (RED) THAT DELIVER, AND VEINS (BLUE) THAT REMOVE, BLOOD FROM THE ARMS AND HANDS.

network of blood vessels carries blood on the round trip to every nook and cranny of the body, and then back to the heart.

Arteries carry blood away from the heart under high pressure, with each heartbeat. Luckily, artery walls are both strong and elastic. With each surge, the walls bulge outwards and then spring back. You can feel this bouncing action where an artery comes near the surface of the skin, especially if it passes over a bone, like it does in your wrist just below the thumb. Each surge or pulse represents one heartbeat. Can you find your pulse? By keeping a finger on it, you can measure your heart rate.

Arteries branch all over the body, eventually leading into microscopic vessels called capillaries. These capillaries are so small that red blood cells sometimes have to bend sideways to fit inside them. Capillaries pass right by cells so that food and oxygen can pass from the blood and into the cells.

Back to your heart

Having done their job, the capillaries link up to form veins that carry oxygen-poor blood back to the heart. Veins have thinner walls and the blood travels through them with only a small amount of pressure. Valves stop blood flowing backwards. Veins take blood back to the heart to begin another trip around the circulation system.

LOG ON..
www.bbc.co.uk/
science/humanbody/

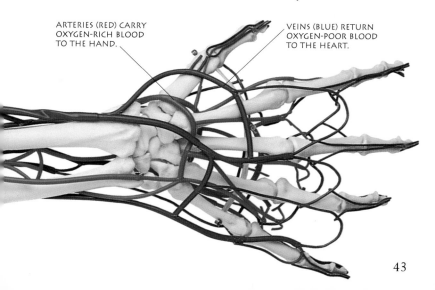

ARTERIES (RED) CARRY OXYGEN-RICH BLOOD TO THE HAND.

VEINS (BLUE) RETURN OXYGEN-POOR BLOOD TO THE HEART.

FOOD PROCESSOR

You probably eat meals about three times a day. What happens between the food going into your mouth and waste coming out the other end? The answer is digestion. As food travels along your tubular guts, it is broken down and digested to release all the nutrients you need to keep you alive and healthy.

Necessary nutrients

What have you had to eat today? Some deep-fried grasshoppers or a few juicy caterpillars in tomato sauce? You might turn your nose up at these food items, but they are firm favourites in some parts of the world. What's more, they are as packed with nutrients as pizza and salad.

What are these vital nutrients? Carbohydrates and fats give you energy. Proteins help you grow and carry out body repairs. Vitamins, such as vitamin C, and minerals, such as iron, keep your cells working smoothly and you healthy. Fibre from fruit and vegetables gives your intestines a work-out to keep them digesting properly. And last, but not least, water keeps you wet inside – among other jobs – and stops you drying up like a wrinkled prune.

Energy from food

Running, talking, even sitting still, are all activities that need energy. That energy comes from food, especially sugars and other carbohydrates.

How much energy you need depends on your age, sex, and what you do. A female athlete, for example, will need more energy than a woman who sits in an office all day. If you use the same amount of energy that you eat, your weight stays the same. People who eat more than they need store the extra energy as fat and get heavier.

GRASSHOPPERS CAN MAKE A HEALTHY MEAL.

NUTRIENTS ARE RELEASED FROM FOOD WHILE IT IS IN THE DIGESTIVE SYSTEM. THIS INCLUDES THE STOMACH (BLUE) AND THE SMALL INTESTINE (GREEN).

45

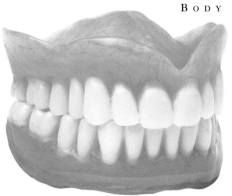

THESE FALSE TEETH SHOW INCISORS, CANINES, PREMOLARS, AND MOLARS.

carefully and you'll see the whole chewing process in living colour!

S lippery swallow

Everywhere in the digestive system, thick, slimy mucus makes it easy for food to slip along the tubes. Mucus is certainly important when it comes to swallowing. Once food has been chewed into a ball, your tongue pushes it backwards. The second it hits the throat, it is automatically pushed down a tube called the oesophagus. Here a wave of muscle

M any teeth

The first stage of digestion is to get food inside your body. Unlike pythons, humans can't swallow their food in one big

BORBORYGMI IS THE SOUND-ALIKE NAME FOR DIGESTIVE NOISES

lump. Instead, we use our toothy tool kit to chop up food into pieces small enough to be swallowed. Incisor and canine teeth at the front of your mouth grab and cut up food. Big, flat pre-molars and molars at the back crush and grind. While the jaws are chomping, salivary glands squirt juicy saliva into the mixture, and your tongue mixes it all up. Usually your lips close to stop the food falling out but, if you have a friend who eats with their mouth open, look

contractions squeezes food down to your stomach, in the same way that you'd squeeze a tube of toothpaste. The whole thing takes just 10 seconds.

C rush to a mush

Imagine taking your favourite meal, putting it into a blender, and whizzing it into a mush. That soupy slop is just what your meal would look like after it had been crushed and churned by your stomach. Chewed-up food arrives from the oesophagus and is

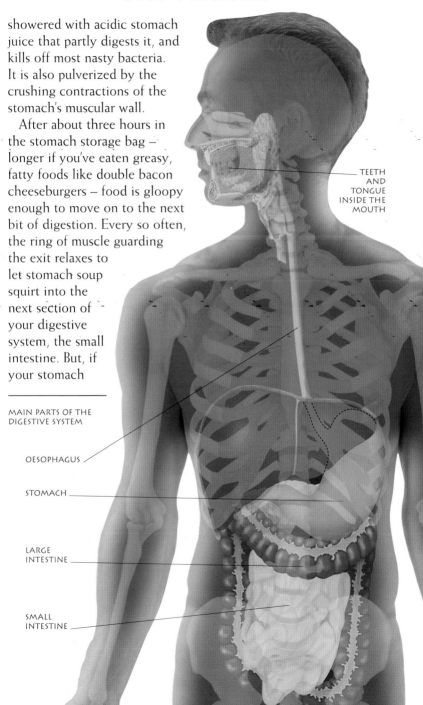

showered with acidic stomach juice that partly digests it, and kills off most nasty bacteria. It is also pulverized by the crushing contractions of the stomach's muscular wall.

After about three hours in the stomach storage bag – longer if you've eaten greasy, fatty foods like double bacon cheeseburgers – food is gloopy enough to move on to the next bit of digestion. Every so often, the ring of muscle guarding the exit relaxes to let stomach soup squirt into the next section of your digestive system, the small intestine. But, if your stomach

TEETH AND TONGUE INSIDE THE MOUTH

MAIN PARTS OF THE DIGESTIVE SYSTEM

OESOPHAGUS

STOMACH

LARGE INTESTINE

SMALL INTESTINE

rejects what you've eaten, it might make you throw up by propelling the liquid food back up your oesophagus and out of your mouth. Try not to be sick over your bike, because the stomach acid in vomit will strip the paint off!

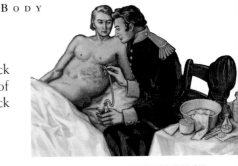

WILLIAM BEAUMONT EXPERIMENTING ON ALEXIS ST MARTIN'S STOMACH.

Inside the stomach

Thanks to a gruesome accident, US surgeon William Beaumont pioneered understanding of how stomachs work. In 1822 he treated seriously wounded Alexis St Martin who had accidentally shot himself in the side. St Martin survived, but was left with a bullet hole into his stomach. For years – even when St Martin objected – Beaumont carried out experiments on St Martin's stomach including dangling different types of food through the hole to see if they would digest. Beaumont's holey observations made him famous.

VILLI INSIDE YOUR SMALL INTESTINE SOAK UP FOOD AND TAKE IT TO YOUR BLOOD.

Small intestine

It seems a bit odd to call the small intestine "small" when it's the longest bit of your digestive system – it's called "small" because it's much narrower than the large intestine. Fortunately it's all coiled up inside the abdomen. If it wasn't, you would have to be a towering 6.5 m (21.3 feet) tall to fit it in.

When soupy food arrives from the stomach it is bombarded with digestive juices again. These juices contain lots of chemical digesters called enzymes that break food down into small useful bits like glucose and amino acids. Digested nutrients swirl around tiny villi, the mini-fingers that cover the inside of the small intestine. These vital villi soak up all the digested food and transfer it into the blood ready for speedy distribution to body cells.

Parasites

At one time, due to poor hygiene, it was common for parasites like enormously long, ribbon-like tapeworms to live in people's guts. These uninvited guests wallow in the soupy food inside the small intestine, and simply soak it up.

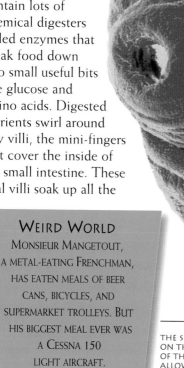

THE SUCKERS ON THE "HEAD" OF THIS TAPEWORM ALLOW IT TO CLING TO YOUR INTESTINES.

WEIRD WORLD

MONSIEUR MANGETOUT, A METAL-EATING FRENCHMAN, HAS EATEN MEALS OF BEER CANS, BICYCLES, AND SUPERMARKET TROLLEYS. BUT HIS BIGGEST MEAL EVER WAS A CESSNA 150 LIGHT AIRCRAFT.

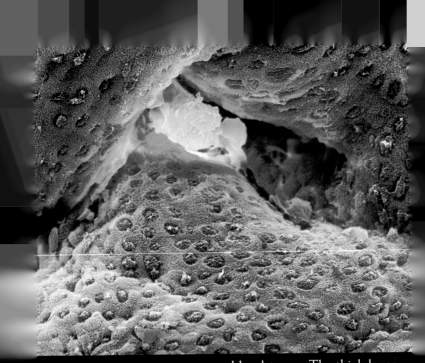

THE LARGE INTESTINE ABSORBS WATER FROM ANY UNDIGESTED FOOD.

Hooks and suckers help tapeworms latch onto the small intestine wall so they aren't swept away. Luckily, better public health and cleanliness has meant that few people get worms from food these days.

Faecal factory

Faeces, the brown bits that come out when you defecate, or go to the toilet, are made in the large intestine. When a liquid delivery of undigested food arrives in your large intestine it really changes. It dries out, as much-needed water is returned back to the bloodstream. The thick layer of "friendly" bacteria lining the large intestine breaks down any food remnants to release the gases that make farts, as well as substances like skatole and indole that give faeces their smell, and the brown stuff that – well – gives faeces their colour. Between 24 and 48 hours after you swallowed that meal, squashy faeces arrive in the rectum at the end of the large intestine. A message from here to the brain tells you that it's time to visit the toilet.

Upset tummy

While faeces are supposed to be nice and chunky, sometimes they are watery and runny.

Having diarrhoea can be a bit embarrassing because it often makes you need to go to the toilet immediately. Diarrhoea usually happens because you have eaten or drunk something contaminated with nasty bacteria. The body likes to get rid of it as quickly as possible.

T yphoid Mary

Getting diarrhoea was a strong possibility if you ate food cooked by

job to job. Finally, in 1915, Mary was arrested and locked away for the rest of her life. Typhoid Mary's reign of terror and tummy trouble was over.

There is always a risk that food

or drink may contain nasty bacteria, such as salmonella. These bugs use the digestive system as a way of getting inside your body. But despite the risk, we have to eat, drink, and digest to survive.

Mary Mallon – a New York chef in the early 1900's. Everyone loved her cooking. What they didn't know was that she carried and passed on a nasty disease called typhoid. As well as causing really bad diarrhoea, typhoid can kill.

As her employers and their families fell ill or died, Mary just moved from

DEEP BREATH

Take a long deep breath. Easy isn't it? Most people breathe in and out without thinking. When you breathe, oxygen races into your body and extracts energy from food, giving your cells power to do their important job. Taking in oxygen is the main role of the respiratory system, and without it we would die.

Oxygen supplies

Earth's atmosphere contains the gas – oxygen – which we need to stay alive. We automatically breathe in air containing oxygen through our mouth and nose – even when we're asleep.

This is all very well at ground level, but there are some places where there is not enough oxygen to support human life. For example, when mountaineers climb to high altitudes, the amount of oxygen decreases dramatically, and they need to breathe through masks connected to cannisters of oxygen. A similar situation applies to scuba divers.

Oxygen for energy

Wherever you are, at this very moment inside your cells, tiny sausage-shaped mitochondria are using up oxygen. Why? To release energy stored in the glucose that you ate in recent meals. This energy powers the activities that keep your cells alive, and also keeps your insides warm. Carbon dioxide is produced as a waste.

Breathing in and out

For this important process to happen, your body has to

MITOCHONDRIA (GREEN) USE OXYGEN TO RELEASE ENERGY FROM FOOD.

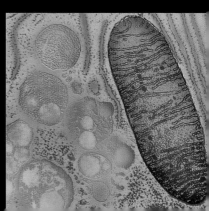

breathe air into your left and right lungs. They fill most of the space inside your chest. Breathing brings fresh supplies of oxygen into your lungs, and flushes out unwanted carbon dioxide. The body bits responsible for doing this are two lots of muscles – the diaphragm, a big sheet of muscle just below the lungs, and the rib muscles. When both

contract, the ribs move up, the diaphragm down, and the space inside the chest increases, sucking air into the lungs. When the muscles relax and the space reduces, air is squeezed out of the lungs and you breathe out.

S oft lungs
Lungs are not hard and solid, as you might expect,

MAIN PARTS OF THE
RESPIRATORY SYSTEM

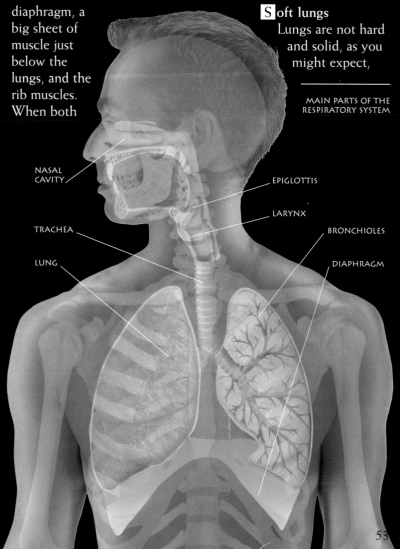

NASAL CAVITY

EPIGLOTTIS

LARYNX

TRACHEA

BRONCHIOLES

LUNG

DIAPHRAGM

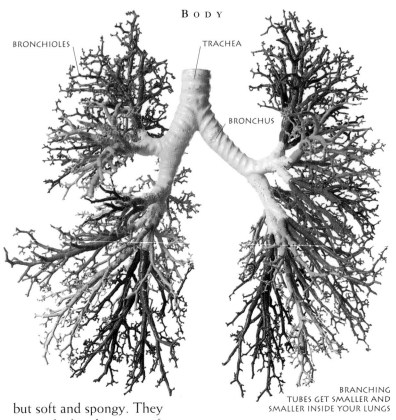

BRONCHIOLES

TRACHEA

BRONCHUS

BRANCHING
TUBES GET SMALLER AND
SMALLER INSIDE YOUR LUNGS

but soft and spongy. They are packed with masses of tubes that branch out from the bronchus, carrying air into each lung. The tiniest tubes inside your lungs – called bronchioles – end in microscopic air bags.

The name given to these air bags – and, no, it's not a type of pasta – is alveoli. Oxygen passes through the alveoli's paper-thin walls before being whisked away by the blood to the body's cells. In exchange, carbon dioxide goes in the opposite direction from the blood to the air inside your alveoli. Then you breathe it out. Gas exchange is no small scale operation. It's happening right now in the 300 million alveoli inside your lungs.

B reath control

As with most body bits, the brain is the control centre. Your brain stem – where the brain joins the spinal cord – keeps you breathing in and out between 12 and 18 times a minute when you aren't doing much. If you start running, you breathe faster and deeper to get more oxygen into your body to release extra energy.

What a yawn!

Sometimes you may feel tired and yawn. No-one's quite sure why one yawning person in a

nose has a built-in filter system. The sticky mucus layer inside traps particles. If you've ever spent time in a dusty room and then blown your nose, you'd see the stuff your nose has filtered from the air.

SPREAD OUT, ALVEOLI WOULD COVER ONE THIRD OF A TENNIS COURT

room sets off everyone else. But we think we know why you yawn. If you are bored or tired, your breathing slows down, and the level of carbon dioxide inside you increases. This triggers a really deep, open-mouthed breath – hand over mouth, please! – that flushes carbon dioxide out of the lungs and gets lots of fresh oxygen in. Unfortunately, if it's a really boring lesson, even a good yawn may not stop you dropping off.

Trapping dirt

All that breathed-in air carries dust, dirt, and germs like bacteria and viruses. Any of these could damage delicate bronchioles or alveoli, so your

No smoking

The nose filter is not much help when it comes to cigarettes, because people smoke with their mouth. Smoke particles go directly to the lungs where they irritate tubes and air bags, and may cause lung cancer. Gases in

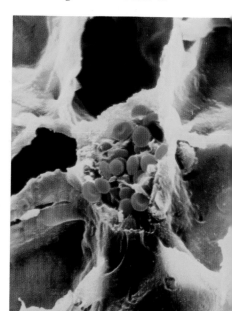

CROSS-SECTION OF ALVEOLI AROUND A BLOOD VESSEL. RED BLOOD CELLS INSIDE THE VESSEL COLLECT AND DISTRIBUTE OXYGEN.

cigarette smoke lower the amount of oxygen carried by red blood cells so smokers get breathless easily. And nicotine in cigarettes makes bronchioles narrower, so less air gets in and out of the lungs. Some very good reasons not to smoke!

S tethoscope

Doctors can find out what's wrong with someone's breathing by listening with a stethoscope. It was French doctor René Laennec (1781–1826) who first came up with the idea. In Laennec's day, doctors had to put their ear right next to the patient's chest to hear them breathing. This could be embarrassing, and also a bit smelly if the patient hadn't washed! Laennec found that

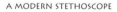

A MODERN STETHOSCOPE

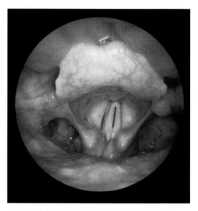

AIR RUSHING THROUGH CLOSED VOCAL CORDS MAKES THE SOUNDS OF SPEECH.

listening to the chest through a wooden tube not only avoided these problems but also made the sounds clearer. Laennec's wooden-tube stethoscope remained popular until 1852 when the modern version was invented.

M aking sounds

One part of the respiratory – breathing – system lets you speak or sing. You can feel the larynx, or voice box, at the front of your neck – it's the bumpy bit. Speak and you'll feel it vibrate. Stretched across it are two vocal cords. If they close, air rushing up from the lungs makes them vibrate and produce sounds. Your tongue and lips turn sounds into understandable words. Keep

WEIRD WORLD

THE WORLD RECORD FOR HICCUPS IS HELD BY AN ENGLISH WOMAN WHO HICCUPED NON-STOP FOR 2 YEARS, 35 WEEKS, AND 3 DAYS DURING THE 1980'S. IN THE FIRST YEAR ALONE, SHE HICCUPED ONE MILLION TIMES.

your tongue still and try to speak. It doesn't work very well, does it?

Choking and hiccups

Speaking and eating don't go very well together and can make you choke. A flap called the epiglottis normally folds over the larynx when you swallow to stop food blocking your windpipe. But sometimes things go wrong, especially if you eat quickly and talk a lot. Unable to breathe, you start to choke. If this happens you automatically cough, and this normally clears the blockage. A slap on the back may help too!

Eating too quickly can also trigger hiccups. A sudden contraction of the diaphragm sucks air into the lungs and makes the vocal cords smack shut to produce a loud "hic" noise. Normally hiccups don't last very long, especially if you hold your breath.

Explosive sneeze

Everyone gets a nose irritation from time to time. Dust or cold irritants trigger an automatic reflex action – the sneeze – that rapidly clears the nose. Sneezes happen like this. You take a deeper-than-normal breath, then send an explosive blast of air up through your nose. Droplets of watery mucus burst outwards through your nostrils at speeds that can reach 160 kmh (100 mph). Bad luck for the person standing right in front of you! This is just one way your body keeps your respiratory system healthy.

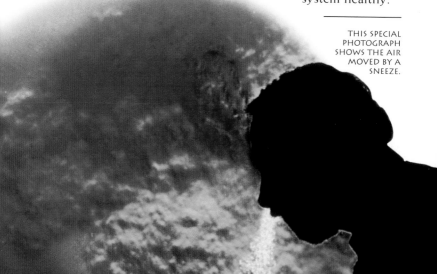

THIS SPECIAL PHOTOGRAPH SHOWS THE AIR MOVED BY A SNEEZE.

BALANCING ACT

Your body's cells work best when the conditions around them are perfectly balanced. Never too hot or too cold, just enough water, and the right amount of food and oxygen. Helping to maintain this balance is the job of the urinary system, as well as the body's temperature regulators, and your hormones.

Urine makers

Making urine is the job of your two kidneys. Day and night they filter the blood to remove any excess water you might have drunk or eaten so that your blood doesn't get too diluted. They also remove unwanted waste, particularly stuff called urea that is made in the liver – a big organ that sits in your upper abdomen, near your stomach. It has about 500 different functions, mainly concerned with processing blood to make sure it contains the right ingredients.

The urine that you get rid of several times a day is made up of water and waste. How much urine you release varies from day to day. So if it's very hot and you sweat a lot, you make less urine. If it's cold and you have lots to drink, you make more.

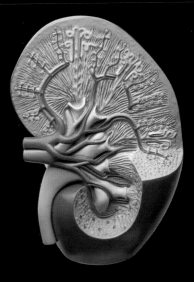

SECTION THROUGH A KIDNEY

Full to bursting

Three cheers for the bladder. Without it you would spend all day sitting on the toilet. Why? Because your kidneys produce a constant trickle of urine that runs into tubes called the ureters. Fortunately, instead of

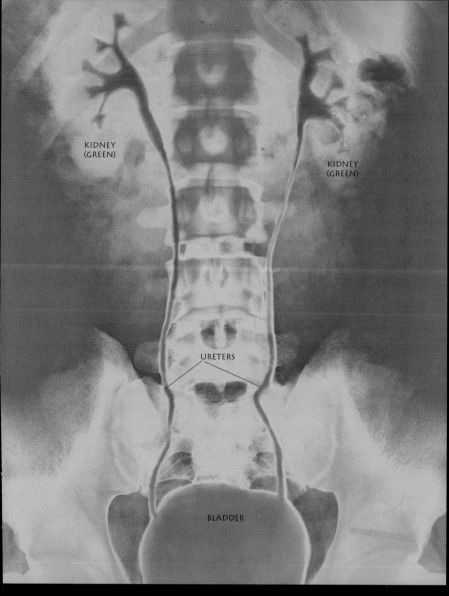

KIDNEY
(GREEN)

KIDNEY
(GREEN)

URETERS

BLADDER

releasing a non-stop stream to the outside of the body, the ureters empty into the bladder. At the base of this storage bag is an opening to the outside, normally kept closed by a ring of muscle called a sphincter. As

KIDNEYS (GREEN) MAKE URINE THAT TRICKLES DOWN THE URETERS TO THE BLADDER (ORANGE).

the bladder fills with urine, its muscular walls stretch and send messages to your brain. You gradually become aware that your bladder will soon need emptying. If you put it off, the feeling gets stronger and stronger until... you can delay no longer, get to the toilet, and relax that sphincter muscle.

Urine test

Be thankful that you weren't a doctor in medieval times. Examining urine was one of the most important ways they had of finding out what was wrong with their patients. That meant not only looking at the colour of the urine sample, sniffing it, and seeing if it was cloudy, but also – yuk! – tasting it. Modern doctors still do urine tests to help make a diagnosis, but luckily they are no longer required to taste it.

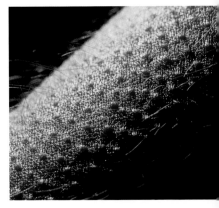

GOOSE PIMPLES OCCUR WHEN YOU'RE COLD. YOUR HAIRS LIFT UP TO TRAP BODY HEAT.

drank (input), and his faeces and urine (output), and himself. Sanctorio noted input was always greater than output, and suggested the difference was due to "insensible vapours". We know now that it was

YOUR BODY IS MADE UP FROM ABOUT 60 PER CENT WATER

Sanctorio's input and output

One man who certainly had urine and balance on his mind was the Italian medical professor Sanctorius Sanctorio (1561–1636). For an amazing 30 years of his life – awake and asleep – Sanctorio spent as much time as possible sitting on a special weighing machine called "The Ballance". Daily he weighed whatever he ate and

caused mainly by water loss during sweating.

Temperature control

Sweating is part of the body's temperature control system. Chemical reactions going on inside your body cells constantly churn out heat. The layer of fat under your skin – and your clothes – also help to keep you warm.

When it's really cold, you probably get little bumps all over your skin – called goose pimples. You may also shiver. By suddenly contracting in a shivering shudder, your muscles release extra heat inside your body, and help to warm you up.

On the other hand, if it's very hot, blood vessels in your skin widen to make them give off heat more quickly, like a radiator. Sweat glands pour lots of watery, salty sweat onto your skin's surface. This evaporates – turns into water vapour – by sucking heat from the skin, so the body cools down. All these things help keep your body at a constant temperature of 37°C (98.6°F).

at that constant level. You can't afford to lose water without replacing it. Luckily, part of your brain called the thirst centre realizes when your blood's getting too concentrated and tells you to have a drink. Drinking liquids replaces most of the 1–2 litres (1.7–3.5 pints) of water you lose each day. But you also get water from food, and not just squashy things like melons or cucumbers.

LOG ON...
www.yucky.kids.
discovery.com/body

Hormones

Another part of the body's balancing act is played by hormones. These are chemicals

Water loss

Sweating is not the only way you lose water from your body. Every time you go to the toilet you release water in urine and/or faeces. When you breathe out, tiny droplets of water vapour escape from your mouth and nose.

But, more than half your body is water, and it needs to stay

BREATHING ON A MIRROR SHOWS THE WATER VAPOUR YOU BREATHE OUT.

that make you become a boy or girl, grow, help you avoid danger, give birth (females only), and keep lots of other life functions in balance. Often called chemical messengers, most hormones are carried by the blood to particular target areas of the body where they have their effect.

They're mostly made by glands – a general name for body parts that make chemicals – called endocrine glands. Hormone headquarters are found in the pea-sized pituitary gland which hangs from the bottom of the brain. This releases lots of hormones that either have an immediate effect, or that tell other hormone-making glands what to do.

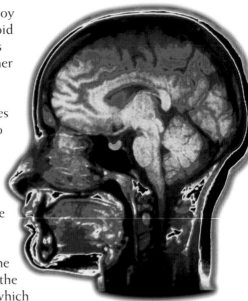

YOUR PITUITARY GLAND (GREEN) IS THE HORMONE HEADQUARTERS OF YOUR BODY.

Sugar levels

Hormones have very important jobs. One of these jobs is linked to glucose, which none of us can do without. Glucose is the fuel we get from food that gives us the energy to stay alive. For that reason it's important to keep a constant level of glucose circulating in the blood. Regardless of whether you're starving hungry or have just eaten, every cell needs to have a non-stop supply.

Making sure that glucose is constantly on tap is the job of insulin and glucagon, two hormones released by the pancreas (just under your stomach). Glucagon increases blood glucose levels, while insulin brings them down, so between them they keep the levels correct.

F ight or flight

Pounding heart, deep breathing, butterflies in the stomach, clammy hands, and knees a bit shaky. Recognize the feeling? People experience it when they are alarmed or frightened by something. It's set off by the hormone adrenalin which prepares the body for stress

THE DANGERS OF EXTREME SPORTS SUCH AS ROCK CLIMBING CAN CAUSE AN ADRENALIN RUSH.

or danger. If the brain thinks the body is threatened – whether its the sight of a charging bull, or climbing a sheer rock face high above the ground – it sends an express message to the adrenal glands. These sit on top of your kidneys and, when told to by the brain, release adrenalin into the bloodstream. Unlike most other hormones, adrenalin's effects are quick and short-lived. By speeding up heart rate and breathing, it gets more food and oxygen to your muscles. That way, you are ready to fight your way out of danger or run away as quickly as possible.

63

SKIN DEEP

Without skin you would look very red and gory. So it's a good job we can't strip off this living overcoat to show off our glistening muscles underneath. Skin, along with hair and nails, marks the boundary between your insides and the outside world, and much more. It keeps out germs and water, filters the sun's rays, and lets you feel textures and surfaces.

Life on the surface

Look closely at the surface of the skin – a microscope helps – and the first thing you notice is that it's bumpy not flat, and has many nooks and crannies. These are packed with loads of bacteria. Most are harmless,

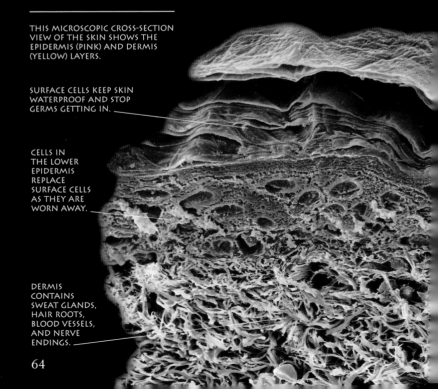

THIS MICROSCOPIC CROSS-SECTION VIEW OF THE SKIN SHOWS THE EPIDERMIS (PINK) AND DERMIS (YELLOW) LAYERS.

SURFACE CELLS KEEP SKIN WATERPROOF AND STOP GERMS GETTING IN.

CELLS IN THE LOWER EPIDERMIS REPLACE SURFACE CELLS AS THEY ARE WORN AWAY.

DERMIS CONTAINS SWEAT GLANDS, HAIR ROOTS, BLOOD VESSELS, AND NERVE ENDINGS.

and do a good job in stopping harmful bacteria – and fungi – from growing on your skin. But they don't stay harmless if they manage to get into the body through cuts or scratches. That's why doctors rub bug-killing antiseptic onto the skin before they give an injection or operate. This helps to prevent bacteria getting in.

Two layers

Dig downwards from the surface, and you'd find your skin is only about 2 mm (0.08 in) thick. That's about as thick as 12 pages of this book. In places with more wear and tear – like the soles of your feet – its usually double that. Your thin skin is made of two layers. On top is the epidermis that waterproofs the skin and stops germs from getting in. Its dead, flat cells are constantly replaced from below as they get rubbed away as skin flakes.

Skin, as well as hair and nails, contains a protein called keratin. The dead cells in the surface layer of the skin's epidermis are packed with keratin. This makes them tough, flexible, and water-repellent, able to carry out their important role until they get worn away as skin flakes.

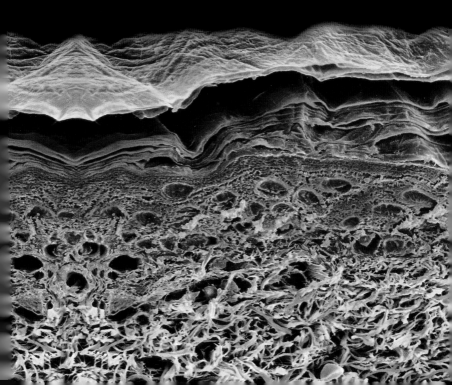

Hair and nails are both derived from the skin, so it's hardly surprising that they, too, are largely made of keratin. So flick a nail, run your fingers through your hair, or touch your skin and you'll feel keratin at work in your body.

Under the epidermis is the thicker dermis. It contains blood vessels, sweat glands, your hair roots, and loads of nerve endings that let you feel pain, touch, heat, and cold.

E xtra padding

Just under your dermis there's a layer of adipose tissue – or fat, as it's usually known. Fat acts as extra padding to protect your insides from knocks and bangs, and works like a living duvet to help keep you warm. It also provides a back-up energy store in the unlikely event that you run out of food. Some people eat more food than they need, and their under-skin fat layer gets thicker, and makes their skin stretch and bulge outwards.

T he big itch

One tiny animal that knows its way around the skin's layers is the itch mite, a microscopic relative of spiders. It's called the itch mite for one very good reason. It causes a disease called scabies that makes people itch so badly they just have to scratch and scratch until their skin bleeds. The male mite is

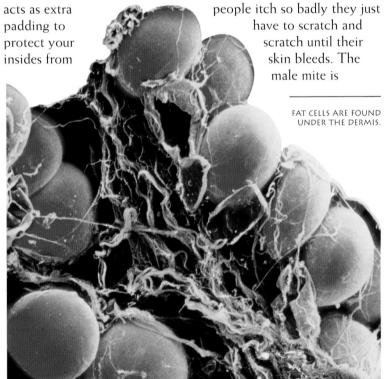

FAT CELLS ARE FOUND UNDER THE DERMIS.

harmless enough. The female, on the other hand, uses piercing mouthparts to dig a burrow through the epidermis into the dermis where she lays her eggs and causes the awful itching. Fortunately for those affected, scabies can be cured using mite-killing lotions.

Skin colour

From the palest pink to the darkest brown, skin colour varies enormously. What colour your skin is depends on the amount of a pigment (colouring) called melanin. This brown-black pigment is made by cells in the epidermis. People with very dark skin produce lots of melanin while those with pale skin produce little melanin. Some people have little patches of skin with extra melanin, better known as freckles. The other thing that colours your skin is the pinkness produced by blood flowing through it. This is less obvious if you have dark skin than if it is pale.

Sun protection

The reason melanin's important is because it screens out harmful rays in sunlight called ultraviolet (UV) rays. That's why people who live in – or whose ancestors originally came from – hot places like

SUN CREAM WILL PROTECT THESE PEOPLE FROM BURNING IN THE SUN'S UV RAYS AND THEIR SKIN WILL GRADUALLY DARKEN.

Ethiopia have darker skin. Their skin naturally produces more melanin for protection from the hot sun than pale-skinned people. Spend time in the sun, and your skin automatically makes extra protective melanin and gives you a suntan. Even so, too much time spent uncovered

WEIRD WORLD
BLEEDING FROM TINY BLOOD CAPILLARIES IN OR UNDER THE SKIN PRODUCES THE FAMILIAR BLACK-AND-BLUE MARKING KNOWN AS A BRUISE. IN TIME, THE BRUISE TURNS YELLOW AND THEN EVENTUALLY FADES AWAY.

under a hot sun – especially if you're not coated with sun protection cream – and the UV rays will burn your skin, causing the painful, hot redness of sunburn.

S pot on

Keeping your skin – and hair – soft and supple is the job of sebaceous glands. These glands release an oily liquid called sebum that lubricates your skin and helps keep it waterproof. That's the good news. Unfortunately, sometimes the tube from the gland gets blocked with sebum, causing spots. If the sebum blockage darkens near the surface, you get a blackhead. Or, the blockage may encourage bacteria to get to work and make things red and infected, in which case you develop acne. Teenagers tend to get spots because their hormones encourage the sebaceous glands to work harder.

WEIRD WORLD

VITAMINS ARE GENERALLY OBTAINED FROM FOOD, BUT ONE – VITAMIN D – IS ALSO MADE BY THE SKIN WHEN IT IS EXPOSED TO SUNLIGHT. VITAMIN D ENABLES THE BODY TO USE CALCIUM TO STRENGHTEN BONES AND TEETH.

A rmpit odours

As if that isn't enough to worry about, you also start to sweat under the arms when you reach puberty. Coiled up in the dermis are the sweat glands that release cooling sweat onto the skin's surface when you are hot. The ones in the armpits release a slightly different sort of sweat. Armpit sweat doesn't smell until bacteria feed on it and release substances that are musky and smelly. That's what gives people who don't wash often, or don't use deodorants, a strong smell of body odour.

F ingerprints

Even your fingertips sweat. Touch glass or metal, and you'll see fingerprints – sweat marks left by your fingers. The curves and loops of fingerprint patterns are produced by skin ridges that help you grip things when you pick them up. No two people have the same pattern of ridges, not even identical twins. At the end of the 19th century, someone realized that sweat patterns left at the scene of a crime could be used to identify criminals. Ever since then, fingerprinting has played an important part in crime detection.

Some criminals have tried to remove their fingerprints so that they couldn't be easily identified at crime scenes. The American gangster John Dillinger got two doctors to remove his fingerprints with plastic surgery in 1934. It was a failure, so next he tried dipping his fingers in acid until the ridge patterns disappeared. Ouch! In the end even this didn't work. By the time he was caught by the FBI later that same year, Dillinger's fingerprints had reappeared and he was once again identifiable.

Curly and straight hair

Another distinguishing feature you have is your hair. It can vary in colour, and you can cut, plait, bead, or even shave it off. Hairs grow from holes in the skin called follicles that are dotted around your body apart from your soles, palms, lips and one or two other places. Whether you are naturally curly, wavy, or straight-haired depends on what shape your follicles are. A round follicle makes straight hair, oval makes wavy, and flat makes curly.

Painless haircut

Hairs grow from the follicles as tubes of dead cells which consist mainly of keratin. That's why it doesn't hurt when you have

CLOSE-UP OF A MAN'S SHAVED FACIAL HAIRS

LOG ON...
www.brainpop.com/health/

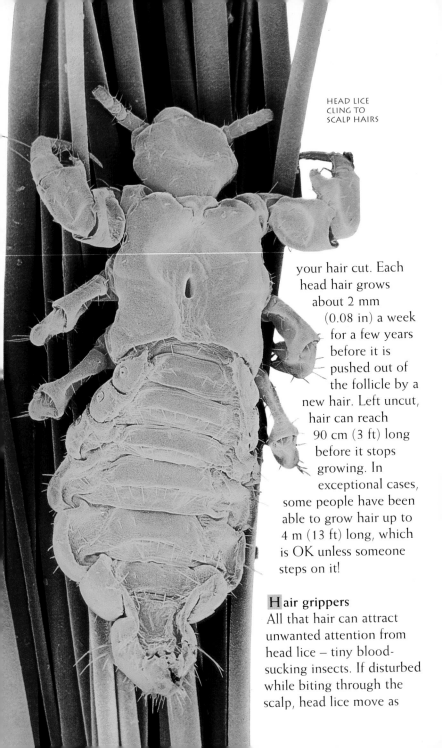

your hair cut. Each head hair grows about 2 mm (0.08 in) a week for a few years before it is pushed out of the follicle by a new hair. Left uncut, hair can reach 90 cm (3 ft) long before it stops growing. In exceptional cases, some people have been able to grow hair up to 4 m (13 ft) long, which is OK unless someone steps on it!

Hair grippers

All that hair can attract unwanted attention from head lice – tiny blood-sucking insects. If disturbed while biting through the scalp, head lice move as quick as a flash, and grab hold of the nearest hair with their "claws" so they don't get dislodged. What's more, female lice actually glue their eggs – called nits – to individual hairs so they don't get swept away when someone washes their hair. Head lice are really common among school children, and they spread like wildfire from head to head. Special shampoos kill off the lice, while fine-toothed nit combs get rid of the eggs.

B ald facts
Some people are not as likely to get head lice because they are bald. For some men,

Nails, also made of keratin, are really useful when have an itch to scratch, or when you are trying to pick up something small. They grow at about 5 mm (0.2 in)

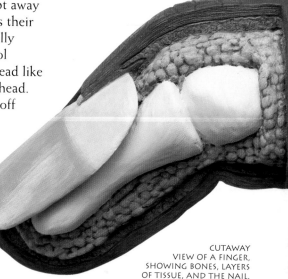

CUTAWAY VIEW OF A FINGER, SHOWING BONES, LAYERS OF TISSUE, AND THE NAIL.

OF THE 100,000 HAIRS ON YOUR HEAD, 80 ARE REPLACED EVERY DAY

the hairs on top of their head grow for such a short time that the hair doesn't even have a chance to emerge above the surface of the skin before it is pushed out by the hair below.

N ails at work
Not everyone has a full head of hair, but everyone has nails.

every month – a bit faster in summer than in winter. Most people cut their nails as they grow. But one man who didn't cut his nails, grew them to over 1 m (3 ft 4 in) long. His thumbnail was the longest nail – it was 1.4 m (4 ft 7 in) long. He obviously didn't work as a painter or dentist!

71

RUNNING REPAIRS

The human body is often referred to as a living machine, and like all machines, it can break down from time to time. If things do go wrong, the body can often repair itself, sometimes with the help of doctors. However, not all illnesses start inside the body. Some are triggered by invaders from outside.

E nemy invaders
Germs or bugs are always hanging about, trying to get inside your body. Those that succeed can make you ill.

are two main types of cells in your blood. Red cells carry oxygen, but white cells do something very different. At the first sign of invasion by

BILLIONS OF HARMLESS BACTERIA LIVE IN YOUR INTESTINES AND SKIN

These pathogens – the proper name for microscopic, disease-causing invaders – include viruses and bacteria. Unluckily for them, your body has a super-strong defence system, and without it you wouldn't last very long. Any pathogens that manage to get in face a deadly army of loyal defenders.

E at and destroy
One of these defenders is your blood. There

pathogens, white cells called phagocytes rush to the site of infection, find the pathogens, and then gobble them up.

PATHOGEN

72

For any pathogens that survive that onslaught, the body has an even deadlier weapon.

This is the immune system, the most sophisticated part of your body's defences. Playing a key role in the immune system are white blood cells called lymphocytes. These long-lived cells keep a record of all the pathogens that have got into your body. If a pathogen

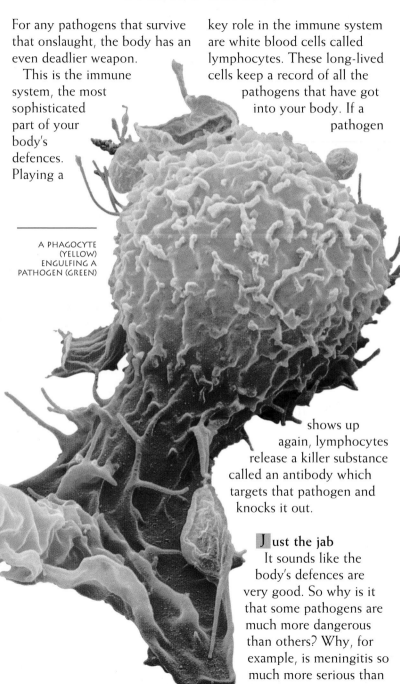

A PHAGOCYTE (YELLOW) ENGULFING A PATHOGEN (GREEN)

shows up again, lymphocytes release a killer substance called an antibody which targets that pathogen and knocks it out.

Just the jab

It sounds like the body's defences are very good. So why is it that some pathogens are much more dangerous than others? Why, for example, is meningitis so much more serious than

73

...he common cold? Well, some pathogens multiply very rapidly inside the body and cause serious illness before the immune system has had time to get its act together. Fortunately, modern medicine has found a way round this.

Doctors can stop people getting a particular disease by injecting a vaccine into their body. A vaccine contains a weak or dead version of the pathogen. This makes the immune system produce antibodies but doesn't cause any illness. If the real pathogen then turns up, it gets wiped out by the army of antibodies that's already waiting there.

Discovering antibiotics

Antibiotics give doctors another weapon in the war against germs. They were discovered by chance in 1928 by Alexander Fleming in London. While studying bacteria, one of his experiments got contaminated with the blue-grey mould you find on rotting fruit. But what really surprised him was that the mould was killing the bacteria.

The bacteria-killing chemical was isolated from this mould, and called penicillin. It was the first of many bacteria-killing drugs, or antibiotics, that have proved to be real life-savers.

Blood clots

Invasion by pathogens is one thing, but what happens if

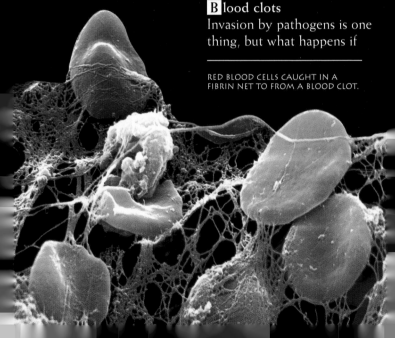

RED BLOOD CELLS CAUGHT IN A FIBRIN NET TO FROM A BLOOD CLOT.

nternal body bits go wrong.
Like a hole in a blood vessel,
for example. Left unrepaired,
blood would just leak out. So
it's a good job the body has its
own pipe repair service.
Whenever a blood vessel is
split or torn, tiny platelets
carried by the blood pile into
the damage zone and "stick" to
each other to plug the leak.

Platelets also do something
else. Sticky platelets release
chemicals that dissolve a blood
protein called fibrinogen into
fibres of fibrin. Just like a
fishing net, these fibres trap red
blood cells and other blood bits
to form a clot that reinforces
the platelet plug. While plug
and clot stop the leak, the
blood vessel wall has time
to rebuild itself.

Fix that fracture

Another built-in repair system
fixes bones if they fracture
or break. Bones are really
strong. But sudden, extra
pressure from an
unusual angle – if
someone falls off
their bike, for
example – can make
a bone break. If
that happens,
bone healing

AN X-RAY OF BADLY
BROKEN ARM BONES.

begins immediately. A clot forms to stop bleeding from the broken ends and new bone grows to join them together. With time, the bone looks as good as new. But fracture mending may need some medical help so the bones heal straight, not bent. To do this, bones may be set in plaster, or have pins put in them.

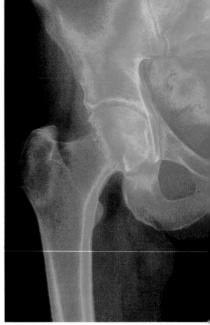

Surgery

Sometimes, the skills of a surgeon are required to fix the body. These doctors operate on the body by cutting into it to carry out repairs. The person being operated on feels no pain because they are given an anaesthetic that makes them unconscious for a while. But this wasn't always the case.

Before 1846 when ether – an anaesthetizing gas – was first used by American William Morton, operations, such as amputations, had to be carried out as quickly as possible. Patients were either tied to the operating table or held down by strong men!

Keeping it clean

A surgeon called Joseph Lister (1827–1912) also improved the chance of surviving surgery. He recognized the importance of keeping clean, and introduced bug-killing chemicals called antiseptics to spray in and around wounds to kill germs. Later on, asepsis was introduced. This involved sterilizing surgical instruments to kill pathogens, cleaning the operating theatre with disinfectant, and wearing clean gowns and protective masks. Just like surgery today.

http://tqjunior.thinkquest.org/5777/

LOG ON...

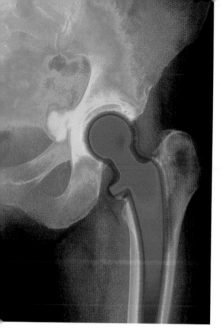

X-RAY SHOWS THE METAL PART (PINK) USED IN A HIP-REPLACEMENT OPERATION.

New body parts for old

Centuries ago, pirates and sailors who had legs or arms blown off in sea battles could replace the missing part with a wooden "peg leg". Things are a bit more advanced now. The latest replacement arms and legs are lifelike and lightweight. Surgeons can operate on the body to replace diseased joints with artificial ones, or worn-out heart valves with metal and plastic replacements. More and more old body parts can be replaced by new ones when needed.

Fit and healthy

In the end, though, you can't beat looking after your body properly so that it only requires the minimum of repairs. A fit body – one that works well – is more likely to be healthy and last longer. Unfortunately, compared to our ancient ancestors, who were forever chasing after antelopes or running away from lions, our modern lifestyle tends to involve much more sitting around, playing with computers, watching television, and eating junk food. So, to keep your body fit it needs daily exercise and a mixed diet that includes plenty of fruit and vegetables and not too much fat.

PLAYING SPORT HELPS KEEP YOUR BODY FIT AND HEALTHY.

77

LIFE STORY

We all follow the same life story. Have you ever heard of a person who has got younger, or anyone who is born at the age of 15? You might want to skip some parts of life, but you can't. We are all born as babies, grow slowly through childhood, change rapidly in our early teens to grow into adults, maybe have children ourselves, and then grow old gracefully.

Frankenstein

Changing the normal life story should be impossible, unless you have the fertile imagination of English author Mary Shelley. In 1818, she wrote a book about a scientist – Victor Frankenstein – who collected bits from dead bodies, and sewed them together to make a new "man". His creation was brought to life using the power of lightning. Frankenstein's monster had a fairly miserable life, and in the end he destroyed the man who had made him.

Race for the egg

In real life, adults who want to make a new human being do it the natural way – by having a baby – not by stitching body parts together. Two vital ingredients are needed –

SPERM CLUSTER AROUND AN EGG, BUT ONLY ONE WILL GET INSIDE TO FERTILIZE IT.

EGG

SPERM

one sperm from father and one egg from mother. While a woman releases just one egg each month from her ovaries, a man makes millions of sperm inside his testes. He releases these inside his partner when the couple become very intimate and make love. Most of the sperm fall by the wayside as they swim madly towards the egg – if there is one – in the fallopian tube that

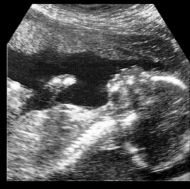

ULTRASOUND SHOWS A BABY GROWING INSIDE ITS MOTHER'S UTERUS.

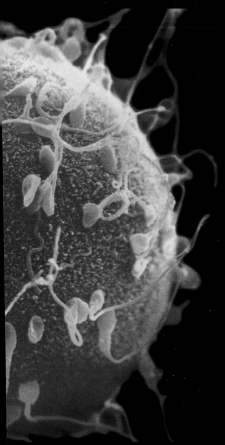

runs between the ovary and the uterus. Of the few sperm that reach the egg, one manages to get inside and fertilize it. A few days later, the fertilized egg has divided to form a ball of cells which sinks into the soft and warm uterus lining and starts to develop into a baby.

Growing inside

It's happened to all of us, although it's doubtful any of us can remember it. The event in question? Being born. Travelling from the warm, quiet, dark surroundings of our mother's uterus and thrust into the bright, noisy outside world with all those people making strange noises. Birth happens about 40 weeks after fertilization. In that short time, we have developed from the microscopic ball of cells that snuggled down in the lining of the uterus, to a 3 kg (6.5 lb) baby with all organs up and running. This includes lungs for loud crying, and fully operative urinary and digestive systems for nappy filling.

It's all in the genes

When a new baby does arrive, it's not unusual for people to say how much she or he looks like her or his mother or father. Are they telling the truth, or not? They very probably are. Every human being inherits two sets of body-building instructions, called genes – one from the mother's egg and one from the father's sperm. Genes interact to make us what we are, with some maternal features, some paternal features, and some that are unique to us as individuals. All these genes – and there are about 30,000 in each set – are strung

along 46 "threads" called chromosomes found in every cell. Chromosomes – and genes – are made of a long molecule called DNA, or deoxyribonucleic acid. DNA molecules contain the instructions, in code, to build and operate each of the cells in your body – and to construct and complete a human being.

Double trouble

Humans usually only have one baby at a time. But not always. Sometimes women have two (twins), occasionally three (triplets) or, even more

rarely, four (quadruplets). So, why do twins happen? Usually, one egg is released each month by one of a woman's two ovaries. But if, by chance, two eggs are released, and both are fertilized by different sperms, they will grow into twins. These twins are not identical because, being made by different eggs and sperms, they don't share the same genes.

SIMPLE MODEL OF A SECTION OF DNA

They could both be girls, both boys, or one of each. Identical twins do share the same genes. They happen when a fertilized egg splits into two separate cells, each of which grows into a baby. They have to be the same sex, and often look so similar that they manage to confuse everybody!

IDENTICAL TWINS ARE FORMED WHEN A FERTILIZED EGG SPLITS INTO TWO TO MAKE TWO BABIES.

L earning zone
Learning about things goes on throughout life, but the busiest time for it is during childhood. Just think of the things you have learned and are learning. How to crawl, walk, run, throw a ball, write, spell, speak, control when you want to go to the toilet... the list is endless. Your brain soaks up information like a sponge, so that you can constantly increase your word power or become better at using a computer. Other

WEIRD WORLD
IN 2000, THE HUMAN GENOME PROJECT IDENTIFIED THE STRUCTURE OF THE GENES INSIDE HUMAN CHROMOSOMES. THAT MEANS THEY'VE TAKEN THE FIRST STEP TO WORK OUT PLANS TO MAKE A HUMAN BEING.

things, like walking or riding a bike, you learn by trying and then using the experience to make improvements.

Growing pains
Once girls are between 9 and 13, and a bit later in boys, big changes happen – puberty has

children look like adults. It also changes the way they think and feel as well.

Old and wrinkly
If you didn't get older, you wouldn't have any birthdays, so life just wouldn't be as much fun. And while it's obvious that

ABOUT ONE IN EVERY 80 BIRTHS PRODUCES TWINS

arrived. This is the time when both girls and boys have a sudden growth spurt, the first time they've grown so quickly since they were babies! Their body shapes change, so they look more like adults, and their reproductive systems "switch on" so they can – when they're ready – have babies.

In charge of these changes are sex hormones. Before you were born, these hormones sorted out whether you were going to be a boy or girl. Now, at puberty, they trigger your body changes.

Puberty is part of adolescence, the growing up process that makes

children grow into adults, you don't really notice signs of ageing until people are in their 40s and 50s. It's around this time that the body's cells start

VERTEBRA THAT HAS BEGUN TO CRUMBLE.

THIS SCAN OF A BACKBONE SHOWS HOW ONE VERTEBRA HAS STARTED TO SHOW THE SIGNS OF AGEING.

getting less efficient. On the outside, the skin gets less elastic and more wrinkly, and the hair gets thinner and can turn grey or white. On the inside, the eyes don't focus quite as well, muscles lose some of their strength, and bones become more brittle. In the end, one or other body system stops working, and the person dies.

However, it's worth remembering that, thanks to good public health and modern medicine, we live much longer than our ancestors did. Good food and plenty of exercise helps as well. Lots of people survive into their 90s and 100s, and – just occasionally – into their 120s.

Into the freezer

Death may be inevitable, but some people still try to avoid it. In recent years it's become possible to pay to have your body deep frozen around the time you die. And deep frozen means just that – a very chilly -196°C (-321°F). The hope is that a deep-frozen body can be defrosted at some time in the future, when doctors know how to cure the disease that killed it. Sounds good, but there are a couple of problems. First, there's no guarantee that the body can actually be woken up from its "frozen sleep". More importantly, would your descendants actually be bothered to unfreeze their ancestors?

LOG ON...

www.genetics.about.com/science
genetics/cs/humangenome/index.htm

A BODY BEING DEEP FROZEN

Well-preserved

Of course, the other way to carry on after death was to get yourself mummified. The mummy experts of the ancient world were the Egyptians. They believed that when you died, your soul left the body, but that they joined up again later. Without a body for the soul to return to, there was no chance of an afterlife. So, the Egyptians used their skills to preserve bodies, although in a rather dried-up form.

People have had their nearest and dearest mummified more recently as well. In Sicily, Italy, there are some 6,000 mummies dating from 1599 to 1920 in an underground cemetery. Wealthy Sicilians had their relatives mummified as a memento of what was once a living, breathing body.

But, however life ends, the path from fertilization to old age is full of change and growth. We each start as a ball of cells, become babies, then children, teenagers, and finally adults, before growing old. This is the body's life story.

RELATIVES CAN VISIT THEIR DEAD, BUT WELL-PRESERVED, FAMILY MEMBERS IN THESE SICILIAN UNDERGROUND TOMBS.

REFERENCE SECTION

Whether you've finished reading *Body*, or are turning to this section first, you'll find the information on the next eight pages really helpful. Here are all the historical facts and figures, background details, body statistics, and unfamiliar words that you will need. You'll also find a list of website addresses – so, whether you want to surf the net or search out facts, these pages should turn you from an enthusiast into an expert.

BODY TIMELINE

c.100,000 BC Modern humans (Homo sapiens) first appear in Africa.

c.70,000 BC Humans spread from Africa to other continents.

c.30,000 BC Cave paintings and sculptures show the shape of the human body.

c.420 BC Greek physician Hippocrates teaches the importance of observation and diagnosis – rather than magic and myth – in medicine.

c.170 Influential Greek doctor Galen describes – often incorrectly – the workings of the body, and his ideas remain mostly unchallenged until the 1500s.

c.1000 Arab doctor Avicenna publishes medical texts that would influence western medicine for the next 500 years.

c.1280 Arab doctor Ibn An-Nafis proposes that blood flows through the lungs.

1543 First accurate description of human anatomy published by Belgian anatomist Andreas Vesalius.

1628 British doctor William Harvey describes how blood circulates around the body, pumped by the heart.

1663 Italian physiologist Marcello Malpighi discovers blood capillaries.

1672 Dutch doctor Regnier de Graaf describes the structure and workings of the female reproductive system for the first time.

1674 Dutchman Antoni van Leeuwenhoek observes and describes red blood cells, sperm, and skeletal muscle cells using an early microscope.

1691 British doctor Clopton Havers describes the structure of bones.

1796 First vaccination – against smallpox – by British doctor Edward Jenner.

1811 British anatomist Charles Bell shows that nerves are made of bundles of neurons (nerve cells).

1816 French doctor René Laënnec invents the stethoscope.

1846 Ether gas first used as an anaesthetic in surgery by US dentist William Morton.

1848 French scientist Claude Bernard demonstrates the function of the liver, and later shows that body cells need to live in stable surroundings.

1851 German physicist Hermann von Helmholtz invents the ophthalmoscope, an instrument for looking inside the eye.

1860s French scientist Louis Pasteur explains how micro-organisms cause infectious diseases.

1865 Joseph Lister, a British doctor, first uses antiseptic during surgery to reduce deaths from infection.

1882 German doctor Robert Koch identifies bacterium that causes TB (tuberculosis).

1895 Wilhelm Roentgen, a German physicist, discovers X-rays.

1901 Austrian-born US doctor Karl Landsteiner discovers blood groups A, B, AB, and O, and paves the way for safe blood transfusions.

1903 An early version of the ECG (electrocardiograph), a device for monitoring heart activity, is invented by Dutch physiologist Willem Einthoven.

1906-12 British biochemist Frederick Gowland Hopkins shows importance of vitamins in food.

1910 German scientist Paul Ehrlich discovers the first drug used to treat a specific disease.

1921 Canadians Frederick Banting and Charles Best isolate the hormone insulin, enabling the disease diabetes to be controlled.

1928 British doctor Alexander Fleming discovers penicillin, the first antibiotic.

1943 Dutch doctor Willem Kolff invents the kidney dialysis machine to treat people with kidney failure.

1953 Using research by British physicist Rosalind Franklin, US biologist James Watson and British physicist Francis Crick discovers the structure of DNA.

1953 American surgeon John Gibbon develops the heart-lung machine to pump blood during heart surgery.

1954 First use of the polio vaccine developed by US doctor Jonas Salk.

1954 First successful kidney transplant carried out in Boston, US.

1958 First use of ultrasound to check foetus health inside a uterus by British professor Ian Donald.

1967 South African surgeon Christiaan Barnard carries out the first successful heart transplant.

1972 CT (computerized tomography) scanning used to produce images of body organs.

1978 Successful IVF (in vitro fertilization) by British doctors Patrick Steptoe and Robert Edwards results in first "test tube" baby, Louise Brown.

1979 Vaccination finally eradicates the disease smallpox from the world.

1980s Introduction of "keyhole" surgery – using an endoscope to look inside the body.

1981 The disease, later to be named AIDS (acquired immune deficiency syndrome), first identified.

1982 First artificial heart, invented by US scientist Robert Jarvik, is implanted into a patient.

1984 French scientist Luc Montagnier discovers the virus – later called HIV – that causes AIDS.

1990 Human Genome Project is launched to analyse the DNA in human chromosomes.

2000 First "draft" of the Human Genome Project is completed.

BODY SYSTEMS

SYSTEM	FUNCTION
Circulatory system	Pumps blood along a network of blood vessels to transport nutrients and oxygen to cells, and remove their wastes.
Digestive system	Breaks down food into simple nutrients that can be used by the body.
Endocrine system	Releases hormones (chemical messengers) into the blood which control several body processes.
Immune system	Defends the body against the bacteria and viruses that cause diseases.
Integumentary system	Consists of the skin, hair, and nails, that cover and protect the body.
Lymphatic system	Drains fluid (lymph) from the tissues from which it filters out pathogens.
Muscular system	Moves and helps support your body.
Nervous system	Controls and co-ordinates the body, and enables a person to think and feel.
Respiratory system	Carries oxygen from the air into the blood, and removes waste carbon dioxide from the body.
Skeletal system	Supports the body, protects internal organs, and permits movement.
Reproductive system	Enables humans to produce children.
Urinary system	Removes waste materials and excess water from blood to be released as urine.

AMAZING FACTS

Cells
• 3 billion body cells die and are replaced every minute.
• Cells lining the small intestine are worn way after 3 to 6 days.
• Red blood cells are worn out by the time they are 120 days old.
• Liver cells live for about 18 months.

Skeleton and muscle
• An adult has 206 bones but a newborn baby has more than 300.
• The body's bulkiest muscle is the gluteus maximus in the buttocks.

Nervous system, brain, senses
• A nerve impulse takes just one-hundredth of a second to travel from big toe to spinal cord.
• Although the brain makes up just 2 per cent of body weight, it receives 20 per cent of the body's blood supply at all times, whether the body is at rest or exercising.

Circulatory system
• A drop of blood has 250 million red blood cells, 16 million platelets, and 375,000 white blood cells.
• The heart beats nearly 3 billion times in a lifetime without ever stopping to rest.
• Stretched out, one person's blood vessels would go round the Earth two and a half times.
• The biggest artery – the aorta – is 2,500 times wider than the smallest capillaries.

Digestion
• Tooth enamel contains no living cells. If it's damaged it cannot be replaced, except by a filling.
• In an average lifetime, a person eats 30 tonnes of food.
• On average, people release enough farts each day to fill a party balloon.

Breathing
• On average, a person breathes in and out about 25,000 times a day.
• The left lung is smaller than the right lung because it has to fit around the heart.

Urinary system
• Daily, the kidneys filter 180 litres (40 gallons) of fluid from blood but produce just 1.5 litres (0.33 gallons) of urine.
• In a lifetime, a person releases 35,770 litres (7,870 gallons) of urine.

Skin
• About 50,000 tiny flakes drop off the skin every minute.
• Fingernails grow four times faster than toenails.
• Itches are caused by irritating dust particles getting into hair follicles.

Body defences
• The eyes blink on average about 9,400 times a day.
• Tears contain a chemical called lysozyme that kills bacteria on the surface of the eye.
• More than 10 billion white blood cells are produced daily to destroy invading pathogens.

Reproduction
• A man's two testes produce more than 300 million sperm every day.
• When girls are born, they already have more than a million eggs present in their ovaries.

BRANCHES OF MEDICINE

Anatomy The structure of the body and how its parts fit together

Biochemistry The chemicals in and around body cells, and how they react with each other

Cardiology The heart and blood vessels, and their diseases

Cytology The study of cells

Dermatology The skin and its diseases

Endocrinology Endocrine glands and their diseases, and the effects of hormones on the body

Epidemiology How diseases are caused and spread within and between groups of people

Gastroenterology The digestive system and diseases

Genetics Genes, chromosomes, and inheritance

Gynaecology The female reproductive system and its diseases

Haematology The study of blood, and diseases affecting blood and bone marrow

Histology The study of tissues

Immunology The immune system and what goes wrong with it

Neurology The nervous system and its diseases

Obstetrics Pregnancy and childbirth

Oncology The causes and treatment of cancers

Ophthalmology The eye and its diseases

Orthopaedics Bones, joints, muscles, tendons, and ligaments, and how they go wrong

Paediatrics The growth and development of children, and childhood diseases

Pathology The causes and effects of diseases, and the causes of death

Physiology How cells, tissues, organs, and systems work

Psychiatry Mental illness and its treatment

Radiology Use of X-rays and other imaging techniques, to investigate and treat diseases

Urology Urinary system in males and females and its diseases, and the reproductive system in males

BODY WEBSITES

www.bbc.co.uk/health/kids
A general site with lots of body information.

http://bart.northnet.com.au/~amcgann/body
A look inside the human body – body guide and fact sheet.

www. bbc.co.uk/education/medicine/
A website that covers Galen, Vesalius, Harvey, Fleming and others.

www.webgod.net/leonardo/Anatomy/Default.htm
Provides good selection of Leonardo's anatomical drawings.

www.virtualvermont.com/history/gage.html
Provides a full account of Phineas Gage and his accident.

www.metaphor.dk/guillotine/Pages/30sec.html
Dr Beaurieux's account of Languille's beheading.

www.james.com/beaumont/dr_life.htm
About William Beaumont including his work with Alexis St Martin.

www.yahooligans.com/content/ka/almanac/bodyfood/index.html
Body and food – an owner's almanac.

TRADITIONAL MEDICINE

Acupuncture Treating disorders by sticking needles into the skin at particular points to alter the flow of energy or Ch'i through invisible energy channels or meridians.

Aromatherapy Aiding relaxation, or treating disorders, with scented plant oils that are massaged into the body or added to bath water.

Ayurvedic medicine Traditional Indian system of medicine that aims to treat the whole person and prevent illness from occurring.

Chiropractic Relief of pain mainly by manipulating the joints of the backbone.

Herbal medicine Ancient practice of using healing properties of certain plants to treat illnesses. Still plays important part in both traditional Chinese and Indian medicine.

Homeopathy Treating disorders by giving patient a very dilute dose of a remedy that in a full strength dose would produce symptoms similar to the illness that is being treated.

Hydrotherapy Use of water – including whirlpool baths, showers, steam baths – to treat a disorder.

Naturopathy Treatment of the whole person by changing their diet or lifestyle, or by using other alternative therapies, in order to restore the body's "normal balance" and boost its ability to cure itself.

Osteopathy Diagnosis and treatment of disorders of the body's framework – bones, joints, ligaments, tendons, muscles, nerves – by, for example, manipulation, stretching, massage, and exercise.

Reflexology Massaging specific regions of the feet in order to treat disorders of parts of the body that are supposed to be related to those regions.

BODY GLOSSARY

Adolescence
Period during teenage years when children become adults.

Alveoli
Microscopic air bags inside the lungs through which oxygen enters the bloodstream.

Amputation
Surgical operation to remove a part of the body, such as an arm or leg.

Anaesthetic
Drug used by doctors to stop the patient feeling pain during surgery.

Antibody
Substance released by the immune system to combat pathogens.

Antiseptic
Chemical rubbed on the skin to kill germs and prevent infection.

Blood vessel
Tube that carries blood through the body. The main types are arteries, veins, and capillaries.

Carbon dioxide
Gas, produced as a waste product of energy release, breathed out in air.

Cartilage
Tough, flexible material that forms parts of structures, such as the nose and larynx (voice box), and covers the ends of bones.

Cells
Tiny living units that are the basic building blocks of the body.

Cerebrum
The largest part of the brain which enables people to think and feel, and controls body movements.

Chromosome
One of 46 thread-like packages of DNA inside every body cell.

Disease
Breakdown in normal working of the body caused by pathogens or a problem inside the body.

DNA
The chemical found inside chromosomes, containing instructions to build and operate a cell.

Endocrine gland
A gland, such as the pituitary gland, that releases hormones into the bloodstream.

Enzyme
Chemical that greatly speeds up reactions, such as the breakdown of food during digestion.

Faeces
Solid waste that remains after digestion, and is expelled from the body through the anus.

Fertilization
Joining together of the egg and sperm during reproduction.

Gene
Instruction needed to build and run a cell stored in the DNA in chromosomes.

Haemoglobin
Substance that carries oxygen in red blood cells.

Hormone
Chemical messenger produced by an endocrine gland, carried by blood.

Joint
Part of the skeleton where two or more bones meet.

Ligaments
Tough straps that hold bones together at joints.

Melanin
Brown pigment that colours skin

and hair.

Mitochondria
Structures inside cells that release energy from food.

MRI scan
Uses magnetism and radio waves to produce images of the body's insides.

Mucus
Thick, slippery fluid that lines the respiratory and digestive systems.

Muscle
Tissue that can contract and cause movement.

Nerve
Cable-like bundle of neurons that links all body parts to the brain and spinal cord.

Neurons
Nerve cells that make up the brain, spinal cord, and nerves, and carry electrical signals at high speed.

Nutrients
Substances in food that are useful to the body, including carbohydrates, fats, proteins, vitamins, and minerals.

Organ
Major body part, such as the heart or brain, made up of different tissues, with a specific role or roles.

Oxygen
Gas taken from breathed-in air and used by cells to release energy from food.

Pathogens
Disease-causing microscopic organisms such as bacteria or viruses.

Peristalsis
Waves of muscle contraction that push food through the digestive system.

Plasma
Liquid, colourless part of blood.

Puberty
Period during adolescence when the body grows and develops rapidly, and the reproductive system starts working.

Reflex
Automatic action such as swallowing, blinking, or pulling a hand away from a sharp object.

Spinal cord
Column of nervous tissue that relays nerve messages between the brain and body.

Stethoscope
Instrument used to listen to sounds made by body parts, such as the lungs and heart.

Sweat
Salty, waste liquid released onto the skin that helps to cool the body.

System
Group of linked organs that work together to do a particular job.

Tendon
Tough cord or sheet that links muscle to bone.

Tissue
Collection of similar cells that have one particular role.

Transplant
Operation to take an organ or tissues from one person and put them into another.

Ultrasound scan
Image produced by beaming sound waves into the body.

Urine
Waste liquid produced by the kidneys.

Villi
Tiny finger-like projections from the small intestine wall that transfer digested food into the bloodstream.

X-rays
Invisible rays used to produce images of hard parts of the body, like bone.

INDEX

CREDITS

Dorling Kindersley would like to thank:
Dawn Davies-Cook and Joanna Pocock for design assistance; Almudena Diaz and Nomazwe Modonko for DTP assistance; and Kate Bradshaw for editorial help. Thanks also to Chris Bernstein for the index.

Additional photography by:
Geoff Brightling, Andy Crawford, Philip Dowell, John Garrett, Steve Gorton, Dave King, Time Ridley, Clive Streeter, Adrian Whicher, Jerry Young.

Richard Walker would like to thank:
Lucy Hurst, Ann Cannings, Fran Jones, Marcus James, and the rest of the team at DK responsible for this book, for their hard work, enthusiasm, creativity, and attention to detail.
